THE LEGACY RULE

Are you helping to create a better future?
That's where all children will live.

BY

JERRY NATHAN

PORTLAND • OREGON
INKWATERPRESS.COM

Scan this QR Code to learn more about this title.

Publisher: Inkwater Press | www.inkwaterpress.com

Paperback
ISBN-13 978-1-62901-134-9 | ISBN-10 1-62901-134-7
Kindle
ISBN-13 978-1-62901-260-5 | ISBN-10 1-62901-260-2

Printed in the U.S.A.

5 7 9 10 11 12 8 6

"To the younger generations – who must undo the mess older generations have made of this planet, but with relevant knowledge and fitting technology made possible by older generations."

Foreword

For various reasons, I have spent my life seeking the best ways to live. Assuming you value sustainable health and peace, consider the conclusions in this book. They are different from where most of corporate America's leaders would take us. We need to aim for a world of diverse people with diverse thinking united in one Earthly community by what we all have in common, our DNA for mutual respect, kindness, and love. Neither opposing narratives, nor opposing ideologies, nor opposing weapons can truly destroy these universal genes. Unfortunately, living in overpopulated habitats covers them up for too many of us and less fully human genetics get expressed. The prevailing immorality in the world today is abuse of power.

Millions are working toward the better DNA world. Their tools are the knowledge that has been generated from social, behavioral, and life sciences, today's communication, education, and information systems, contraception and family planning coupled with a sense of population ethics, and an emphasis on small, local steps of effort and results all over the globe.

The right top-down leadership from government, business, and religious sources could certainly help, but up-to-date knowledge has to be the final word. We must take responsibility to educate and inform ourselves and our home communities and neighborhoods in science-backed ways of health and peace. Only this can transform entire cities, states, and nations into a world all future children deserve.

"The world as we have created it is a process of our thinking. It cannot be changed without changing our thinking." **Albert Einstein**, Physicist, 1879 – 1955.

"Any intelligent fool can make things bigger, more complex, and more violent. It takes a touch of genius – and a lot of courage – to move in the opposite direction." **E. F. Schumacher**, Economist, 1911 – 1977.

How much time (or fortitude) do you have for reading this book? Here are the best places to stop.

The Legacy Rule

The Roots of Sustainable Civilization

Empire-Builders as Obstacles

What Makes Mature People

Note: This book is not pleasant to read – take it seriously enough and you'll feel alarmed or downright depressed (no best seller here). But everyone should know what's in it, especially if younger than 40. To help the cause, I have tried to make most pages stand-alone, mini-essays. Just scanning the headings and reading a few pages here and there can still provide information. However mini-essays about big subjects will be short on examples – more lecturing, generalizing, and repetition – less showing how or why (and there's all the other pertinent stuff I left out). The best long book (to date) on this subject is *Countdown* by Alan Weisman (or maybe *Ishmael* by Daniel Quinn).

Note Too: When I bad-mouth corporate empires, I am not talking about locally-owned incorporated businesses. I also recognize that many stockholder-owned national and multi-national corporations give us products that sustainably improve our health and peace which local groups could not do. And my negative opinions about religious empire-builders are not meant to be against religion. Up-to-date knowledgeable religious people do tremendous good on this Earth.

First Off: Some 50 years ago I read a short anecdote about a missionary or an anthropologist (someone of overpopulated European descent) teaching games to the children of a Southwest Native American tribe. What I remember is that when he wanted them to run races, each and every one (all ages) would make sure that he or she crossed the finish line at exactly the same time as all the rest. No one went faster than the youngest (or slowest) one. They didn't value beating others to some goal. They valued everyone "winning." I never forgot that observation, but I couldn't begin to recall where I found it.

The point here is I am not able to document all the sources of research and information that have gone into my life-time-in-the-making world-view. So, I am not writing this book in a scholarly manner (no citations). I do list the scholars and researchers (page 4) I am familiar with. For the most recent validation of my thinking, I am indebted to the research work of Lester R. Brown, Alan Weisman, Paul K. Piff, Robert Reich, and Thomas Piketty. (You can find them online for a bibliography.)

I have also used some of my own definitions and woven in some of my own "half-baked" theories (it's my book) to make sense out of and link various findings from different sciences. They (my definitions and theories) have not been "peer reviewed." I therefore encourage you to be on the lookout for research data that shoots down any of the supposed insights and ideas herein. So will I – as I always have.

Are you a lifetime learner? If we can't change our minds, why have them. Doubt tests truth. Certainty can keep us bound to error. It is stupid and dangerous to conduct one's life with beliefs that don't fit evolving knowledge of reality.

Don't let your ideologies determine what knowledge you accept. Let knowledge determine what ideologies you accept. And let observation, experience, measurement, data, and logic (the ways of science) determine your knowledge.

My definition of 21st Century civilization: A planet of people universally living at higher standards than ever-present thirst, hunger, chronic stress, ill-health, or danger.

These higher standards don't just happen. People learn how to make them happen and how to keep them sustainable in their cultures. Not just yours or mine, but everybody's children and grandchildren deserve to take their place in a civilization of sustainable health and peace. And, in spite of one exception, realistic habitat populations, we have made tremendous progress in this direction. But the evidence says that one exception has our children currently heading into a world of increasing thirst, hunger, chronic stress, ill-health, and danger.

The danger is coming from massive, human-caused weather disasters (already started), opportunistic diseases (moving in), and such a resurgence of human-generated evils in the fallout that a collapse of civilization is possible in the future. No kidding here – a life-style makeover is necessary for most families, their communities, and their societies or the entire human species on this planet (not just some far-away places) will be back to the most uncivilized conditions before the end of this century.

So far, our recorded history suggests we aren't intelligent enough to maintain a sustainable civilization. "Free-market" capitalism obviously does not do it (look at the Un-united States). Top-down socialism proved not sustainable (think Soviet Union). Agrarian self-reliance has the best track record (4000 years in China), but it too is ending. (Read *The Good Earth* by Pearl S. Buck, also current news stories about forced urbanization there – urbanization puts people in position to be dependent or left out.)

Even our relatively healthy, peaceful hunting and gathering period came to an end after nearly a couple hundred thousand years or more (though most people get it confused with the last ten thousand years of human habitats already overpopulated).

Sustainable Civilization: Civilization that continues without subtracting from each next generation's prospects to live by the same standards.

Why are we failing our youth in this regard? So far, it looks like people born since 1980 (millennials) are the first generation with a majority worse off than their parents. What makes a civilization sustainable?

I think the best answers are gleaned from the works of the following researchers and scholars. I don't agree with everything they say, nor would you, but you would get many times more information about "the big picture" (authentication too) from their books.

Thomas Malthus	John Stuart Mill
Peter Kropotkin	Scott and Helen Nearing
E. F. Schumacher	Rachel Carson
Aldo Leopold	Barry Commoner
Duane Elgin	Kirkpatrick Sale
Herman Daly	Paul L. Wachtel
Joe Dominguez	Vicki Robin
Albert Bartlett	Jim Hightower
Paul Hawken	Wendell Berry
Paul Ehrlich	Anne Ehrlich
Lawrence Lader	David Barsamian
Alan Durning	David C. Korten
Norman Borlaug	Stan Rowe
William Ophuls	Al Gore
John Holdren	Lindsey Grant
Arundhati Roy	Gretchen Daily
Bill McKibben	Ferenc Mate
Jeremy Rifkin	Stephen Emmott
Jared Diamond	Richard Dawkins
Lester R. Brown	Alan Weisman
Paul K. Piff	Thomas Piketty

Even more conclusive (and to the point), you could also read any of the following collections of U.S. and international research studies regarding sustainable civilization.

So far, the U.S. Congressional leadership has mostly ignored them and the majority of voters don't even know they exist. These reports contain the most scientific data and documentation for their conclusions about population.

1954 Hugh Moore Fund Pamphlet
1959 Draper Report
1967 Population Reference Bureau Bulletins
1972 MIT-Club of Rome Publication
1972 The Rockefeller Commission's Findings
1980 The Global 2000 Summary
1985 The World Resources Institute Report
1995 EPA Science Advisory Board Conclusions
1996 President's Council on Sustainable Development Advisory
1997 Jordon Commission Report (and three prior reports)
2004 9/11 Commission Report
2014 U.S. National Climate Assessment Report (three prior reports)
2014 Intergovernmental Panel on Climate Change Report (also five
      prior reports and subsequent reports)

Or

Read this book (at least to page 67). This is my "take-away" after decades of studying what I consider the underlying common cause of our environmental and social ills. Or start on page 116, where I cover psychological consequences of overpopulation on individuals. You might indulge me with the "homework" page (169) and the "final exam" (171). In any case, for the sake of everybody's children and grandchildren, join the millions already working to reverse our collective direction. (You have my respect if you already are.)

Why do civilizations fail? The most basic answer has to be this: no species can keep multiplying indefinitely in a finite habitat (or planet) of finite life-supporting resources. That includes humans.

Environmental demand cannot exceed sustainable carrying capacity. Unfortunately, the dominate species will be the last to know. Dominance provides a false sense of security – the top 20 per cent or so on the world's socio-economic scale think we're mostly doing fine (and the decision-makers of most news media are among them).

Industry and technology give us the illusion that we can figure out how to feed and socialize as many children as get born. The fact is, engineering, no matter how amazing, only buys us a little more time. Most industry and technology now require looting habitats and liquidating resources from species with no voice and from societies with less power to resist. Our numbers are fracturing the entire natural system of life supports and Planet Earth has had enough of our disregard.

Frankly, whether our descendants eat tomorrow, depends on our breeding habits today (if not yesterday). We have made more people than the Earth can handle. There are now over 7 billion of us on the planet and about half of them are under 30 (child-bearing) years of age. That has us heading for 10 billion and probably more, with ever larger numbers of refugees fleeing unlivable conditions to go where?

Thousands of children are dying every day from starvation and around a billion people are malnourished. It's not simply a distribution problem. Some estimates say that 3 billion people will be running short of fresh water by 2025, most of which is used for irrigation to grow food.

More people coming and less food growing takes down civilization. Every species that outgrows its resource base crashes. We have violated this most fundamental law of healthy, peaceful, sustainable civilization. We are on a collision course with this reality.

Consider the surprise factor in these stories.

A farmer has a small pond in which he raises fish to eat. One day, a swimming water bird leaves a speck of living "scum" from his feet on the surface of the pond. The plant-like scum, unless removed, doubles in size each day. Let us say that, given the size of the pond and certain chemical properties in the scum, in 30 days it will cover the entire pond and the fish will all die. After a few days, the farmer notices the scum, knows that he can get rid of it easily, but waits until he is less busy. Most of the pond (7/8ths) is still scum-free when he goes on a three-day trip. When he returns, the fish are all dead.

A logging company leases the timber rights to a vast tract of national forest. As some years go by, a small town develops on its edge to support the loggers (café, grocery store, three bars, etc.) The demand and the price for lumber keep climbing so the company keeps expanding and is able to cut down twice as many trees each year as the year before. Though they know the trees will be gone someday, when the town's people look out and see half the trees still there, most of them don't realize that in one more year there will be none and the company will move on.

These stories illustrate the surprise of exponential growth. We don't realize what's happening until it's too late. The rate of growth is as important as growth itself.

For a long time, the Earth's human population was growing at the average rate of more than four children per couple. Around 1800, it reached 1 billion. By roughly 1920 (120 years), we had doubled that. The next doubling (4 billion) occurred only 50 years later (1980). The next doubling may take a little longer than 50 years, but the problem is we are talking about doubling. That's exponential growth. Most of us know we can't keep adding people forever, but few of us realized that it's the doubling that has been most insidious.

Our over-abundant human presence consuming too many resources in over-developed and developing nations have already caused permanent change to three sub-systems of Earth's life-supports.

They are:

1. Climate change due to global warming – this from too much of our carbon dioxide, methane, and nitrous oxide in the atmosphere. (And major players in the fossil fuel industries are still trying to mislead us.)
2. Biodiversity loss – that's plant and animal extinction mostly due to loss of habitat and pollution, many with their importance to ecosystems and their genetic benefits to humans unknown.
3. The disruption of global nitrogen and phosphorus cycles due to the production and overuse of artificial fertilizers to maximize crop yields. This is wearing out soils and causing dead zones to spread in lakes and oceans.

Our scientists do not fully understand the consequences of our crossing these borders, but they know it's not "pretty."

Other boundaries close to the tipping points for long-term disruptions to life-supporting ecology are our fresh water use (too many people needing it and the food crops it irrigates), land-use changes and deforestation (too much lost to development, erosion, and pollution), and ocean acidification.

Like the atmosphere, the oceans are absorbing too much carbon dioxide from too many people burning fossil fuels. Coral reefs (homes to sea life that support the entire ocean food chain) are being lost twice as fast as rainforests. Ocean plankton, which provides half the oxygen we breathe, is decreasing every single year.

A most fundamental piece of our Earthly life-support system is a moderate climate.

Our climate system has four major components:

1. The atmosphere is the air around planet Earth.
2. The hydrosphere is the Earth's water.
3. The cryosphere is the Earth's ice sheets and glaciers.
4. The biosphere is the Earth's plants and animals.

These four components all interact to maintain a climate with an average range of temperature that supports human life.

Too many people consuming too many resources have now compromised every one of these major components. The atmosphere is holding in too much heat (already the number one killer in large cities). Fresh and potable water is getting scarce. Ice and snow sheets are getting smaller. Plants and animals are rapidly and sadly going extinct, many, many times faster than normal.

The fall-out of our breeding and consuming is changing our climate and that is threatening civilization. The seasons are getting more unpredictable, the storms more extreme, the range of temperatures more wild, while the average is getting warmer. Can we ever grow enough food under these conditions? (Not much food grows above 90 degrees F.) If the numbers of us who burn fossil fuels don't decrease and if the present "burners" don't decrease their usage (and developing countries want to consume like we do), will our descendants be able to survive?

A warming planet, plus shortages of fresh water for irrigation, plus farmland lost to development, plus degrading soils, plus collapsing fisheries, but ever more mouths to feed – who's responsible for this situation? How about our leaders and their followers? How about us? (And in the U.S., we just elected our fourth environmentally illiterate president since 1980.)

The Good News!

We have all the necessary knowledge and technology for the entire world to live sustainably in health and peace. And the necessary changes have been getting promoted by many organizations and implemented by many people for some time (while some never got off track to begin with).

There is currently less violence and killing on the planet than there has been in past centuries (just more news stories about it). More nations in the world have become democratic and more people in the world are getting out of poverty (currently).

The world is experiencing the largest progressive movement it has ever known. It is moving away from unsustainable development with its increasing over-stress, inequality, and environmental ills and in the direction of more sustainable health and peace. Many more people are living more modestly by choice.

Unplanned pregnancies are decreasing. More and more people are choosing to have smaller families. Currently, over 40% of U.S. families have only one child. Nearly half of the world's nations have stable or declining populations. World-wide, the number of children younger than 15 has now stopped rising. About 75% of women are now able to use contraception when they don't want to become pregnant. In fact, the world's average birth rate per woman has been halved since 50 years ago. (That's a slower rate of growth – total numbers of mouths to feed, socialize, and educate are still climbing.)

In the case of global warming, these home-grown efforts at voluntarily and collectively reducing the world's birth rates may be the only way to save ourselves, given the power and wealth addiction in all the corporate empires that "need" to keep fossil fuels burning.

What's not good!

The problem is not enough people were aware of the necessity of smaller families soon enough (that unbelievable, exponential surprise). The problem is not enough contraceptive means and "morning after" pills are being made readily available (a third to half of all pregnancies are still unintended). The problem is people aren't hearing or believing their scientists. Polls show only 10 to 15% of U.S. citizens are even interested in science – compare with sports or fashion (or celebrities).

The problem is that some U.S. Far Right Republican state and federal politicians keep cutting the funding for family planning services, including funds pre-pledged to the United Nations for that purpose. (Reagan started this.) The problem is that old men in the Vatican and in Salt Lake City and in parts of the Middle East, Africa, and Asia, can't bring themselves to endorse modern contraception and smaller families knowing it would slow (or stop) the growth of their religious or political empire. (We must by-pass them.)

The problem is to keep an economy growing profits for corporate investors, they need growing numbers of consumers. The problem is the short-funding of public education with ever growing numbers of students. The problem is not enough decent-paying employment for everyone. The problem is that a scarcity of essentials for living (water, food, and housing), when controlled by corporate empires, makes the rich richer. (They will say "market forces" raise the prices.)

The problem is those who don't fit into the economic system still have needs and many will turn to violence or crime or join gangs of drug runners or extortionists or kidnappers or terrorists when they have nothing more to lose.

The problem is most of us are too busy trying to keep our standard of living or just getting by, when we need to be questioning and demonstrating and voting against the powers profiting mightily from the status quo.

We still have population momentum from earlier generations making families too large for their habitats.

With half of Earth's human inhabitants currently under the age of 30, the world's population will continue to grow when we need to be reducing people pressure on our ecosystems. If we continued at today's rate of births and deaths (2014), we would have 28 billion individuals looking for food by the end of this century. Of course, Nature will stop that long before it happens – if we don't. (Nature will not do it kindly – will we?)

Through education and incentives, we need to reduce the world's population to scientifically-determined carrying capacity. Then we need to average a fertility rate of two children per woman per lifetime (that's average). However, we have many people, especially empire-leaders and followers, who are too invested in the status quo to believe the gravity of the need (or maybe even care). This is especially true in the United States – where today just six private, for-profit corporate media empires control 90% of what people there see, hear, and read. You can bet not much of it is reinforcing the need to reduce the population or grow the economy toward smaller, more local units of production. Some 400 individuals now have as much wealth as the bottom half of this nation's entire population. Around 150 CEOs of huge investor-owned corporate conglomerates control nearly half of global business transactions, exploiting and liquidating the world's resources for profit. Many of the above use their financial clout to keep spreading doubts and fears about changing our direction (and about people who might make changes if elected to public office).

Thus far, change is not happening fast enough on a large enough scale to prevent the hell that is on the horizon (and arriving in parts of the Middle East, West Africa, and Central America at this writing). Sooner or later, every cause is a lost cause unless we turn around population growth.

So, who am I to be bringing up this "gloom and doom" scenario (and saying bad things about "holy" competition too)?

First off, I am not connected to any group that would fire me, excommunicate me, demote or punish me for what I say or write. I do not depend on any empire-building organization for my survival or identity. I have no need to say what will sell. I am free to speak truth as best I understand it. This book is meant as a reality check and reality checks are usually prompted by negative events. I'd rather be wrong, but, if I am to be honest with my self, I have to call it as I see it.

I am an Earthling, a United States citizen, a veteran, a husband, a father, and a grandfather (also an ex-Republican – and, later, an ex-Democrat). I also call myself a naturalist, a garden-farmer, a hair-sheep (healthy meat) rancher, a news junkie,, and a scholar of life-styles. My rural, isolated, childhood was such that I became a misfit mostly lost in the populated adult world and hungry for information about how to carry on. Discovering how to live well in health and peace became my mission in life.

I have made over 75 trips around the sun gravity-glued to my favorite planet. The first half of that journey included the most traveling, studying, and working in various places. All of it included observing, listening, reading, making notes, thinking and getting to know people (as only an introvert can), while advancing and correcting my assumptions and assertions about what makes a good life.

The last half of my life has been living on a small piece of land upon which I can (as necessary) grow and produce my own food and heat with mostly human (and solar) energy. This has been my home base where I am in charge of my life and live my values in keeping with a relaxed (non-competitive) lifestyle. Once I got it paid for, I switched to working part-time and did my best, most satisfying work. I didn't have to "go along to get along." (I did lose a couple of wives over it.)

I was lucky to come of age at a time when my home habitat was not overpopulated.

In my youth, there were many more opportunities in the U.S. for academic learning and for earning livelihood than the average young person has today. In the 1960s, in my home area, jobs were always available. And land-grant public universities still functioned according to their original purpose – provide education for the non-rich, non-elite, non-privileged. If you wanted to become a more knowledgeable person (or get employment with less physical labor – like skinny me), you could work your way through four years of college without amassing a lot of debt (no parents necessary either).

I have a Ph.D. from the University of Nebraska which focused on the science of learned behavior. I was Oregon licensed as both a psychologist and a marital-family therapist. I was also nationally certified as a sex educator and as a sex therapist by the American Association of Sex Educators, Counselors, and Therapists and certified as a sex therapist (and clinical fellow) with the American Board of Sexology. I had a 28-year career in private practice helping clients discover and develop their healthiest habits for living and loving (they go together well). To keep my licenses and certifications, I was required to have 25 hours of continuing education each of those 28 years from scientists and scholars talking about the latest findings on healthy ways to live. I also did occasional college classroom teaching and a lot of searching out research in science journals (plus keeping culturally aware with a daily newspaper and favorite publications: *The Week, The Washington Spectator, The Nation, Mother Jones, Yes! Magazine, Utne Reader,* and *Mother Earth News*).

Given the opportunities that society provided for me, I want to contribute to the public conversation about what I learned. In this book, I am sharing my conclusions about the most crucial objectives for making world-wide health and peace a sustainable reality.

Human nature from my perspective.

Because of evolution, humans have most genes shared by other living beings, especially mammals and most especially primates. So we have genes that support competition and violence and fighting and killing, even infanticide and cannibalism. They are left over from when we were still more animal-like and subhuman. Fortunately, our ancestors didn't stop evolving at this less-than-mature human level. One important change is that they tamed their aggressive instincts through hunting animals for food. Instead of full-blown, muscular attacks, they had to remain calm, use stealth and more brain-power to succeed. They early-on learned to group, cooperate, and share to survive. (Civilization means not having to carry on with our uncivilized genes.)

Collaborative living in small groups allowed their evolution to continue and, because of it, would-be humans developed physical anatomy and physiology for smiling and laughing, enjoying and bonding with each other. Both sexes went on to gain the ability to enjoy sex without waiting for a female cycle of being "in heat." All of this increased interaction resulted in the evolution of physical mechanisms for speech and then an expansion of their language.

Language development, in turn, had them evolve more brain structure for thinking and problem solving and more functioning intelligence. They discovered fire for cooking (tenderizing) meat and fiber. This let them evolve smaller jaws and teeth which provided more skull capacity for their brain development.

Bigger brains and functional intelligence held up until present times when neuroscientists are finding that our brains are getting smaller on average. We now depend so much more on growth-minded leaders (corporate, political, religious) and technology (automation, software, robots) to do our thinking and our work for us. Maybe the easier it is to accomplish something, the less brain development needed (and, I wonder, if less maturing of character too).

We survived our evolutionary history with DNA for voluntary socialism. It became too successful and then we had to compete with each other.

With living in small groups and sharing needs for living, their unrestricted sexuality, their cooperative and giving nature (including keeping the peace with neighboring villages for mutually sexual good times), the population of homo sapiens kept increasing. And, whenever their numbers became too large for their home habitat, the young and the bold (and conflict-avoidant) could migrate into new food-abundant river valleys and seashores and hunting grounds. And so they did throughout their ancestral Africa, into the Middle East, eventually Europe and Asia. A few even made it into a "new" continent, now called the Americas.

Hundreds of thousands of years of relatively healthy and peaceful living occurred before the first natural human habitats got stuck with too many hunters and gatherers. It was 30 or 40 thousand years ago, that some of our ancestral groups had to compete with one another for the same territory and food sources, predisposing them to conflict, fighting and killing. This violent competition became very common by about 10,000 years ago and has been going on, more or less, ever since. We had regressed to less mature behaviors.

We first solved the problem by developing agriculture to increase the food supply. It proved to be temporary; the population exploded after that. The European discovery of a "new" under-populated continent bought some time (at the uncivilized expense of the natives already there). So did applying science and engineering to food-growing and distribution. The results are always the same. More population growth follows.

The problem of overpopulating our natural habitats has never been universally solved. (In fact, the winners of the competition keep developing economic systems based on its continuation – slavery, feudalism, colonialism, free-market capitalism, corporate oligarchy.)

Our competitive cultures have us living below our full genetic endowment.

Competition with each other is said (by promoters) to provide the incentive that brings out our best. It certainly brings up the strongest "intentions" in animals, human or otherwise, if the goal is survival or sexual privileges. The prospect of such loss also brings out more anti-social, unethical behavior, and long-term mistakes. Human beings can do better than that. For living together in sustainable health and peace, they must do better than that.

The main incentives for non-competing originators of worthy creations and ideas come from satisfying their own natural curiosity as they develop their skillset (knowledge, abilities, self-control). Their efforts can also get them appreciation, admiration, and respect from their peers. And that their results can help others is tremendously rewarding (think Jonas Salk with his development of polio vaccine). Plus, a cultural habit of looking out for each other adds to a sense of security and well-being. (How often do competitors look out for each other?)

Humans possess physical attributes and internal chemistry that could not have evolved without coming to each other's aid as well as peaceful socializing (and sexualizing) in and between small communities in natural human habitats for two or three hundred thousand years. That is our full genetic endowment.

The human race is just one race. Underneath our skin, we are all related, one big family, from common ancestors way back. Differences in outward appearance (and digestion) are the result of more recent evolvements as humans emigrated away from our origins leaving their descendants adapted to newer, different environments. We are still all cousins to others of our generation and uncles and aunts to the next. We are all in this together to be caring about one another's welfare and our planetary home. Competition to live decently largely destroys this sense of kinship as it destroys the empathy that supports it.

Competition in human cultures is for sperm, for games of mutual fun, and for the best ideas and creations rising to the top in a cooperative, share and add-on system of social well-being.

Of course, people who believe in their ideas and creations can end up competing with one another as they promote them in any marketplace. Problems in civilization arise when growing overpopulation gets competition so fierce that the power of winning becomes a higher value than following the same boundaries, rules, ethics, facts, truths, etc. as other competitors; we lose the cooperation context. Then, people and their organizations have to be as unethical and untruthful as the least among them to remain competitive. Then, they have to close their minds to new learning. It could show them wrong and weaker. (We even seek out our own "safe" news media.) Discussions become arguments with each side saying whatever might strengthen their position. It weakens the power of language and there is a breakdown of collective trust. We get collective trust only when we can speak (or write) as sincerely and authentically as we know truth and reality to be.

Consider the differences between people having to compete for the opportunity to develop a life of health and peace and everyone having an equal opportunity to do so. How about the differences between people being reared in a competitive society with emphasis on their winning and flaunting more money and privilege than other competitors and a society where the emphasis is on learning and improving one's own fund of knowledge, abilities, and self-control to benefit all of society. Greed is not normally part of human nature. Greed only becomes normalized from the resulting competition and possessiveness in conditions of too many people per natural habitat.

We overbred our habitat populations. Then we overcut, overplowed, overgrazed, overpumped, overfished and overloaded gases into the atmosphere. In our greed, we Earthlings have overshot sustainability.

Competition and cooperation are basically opposing sets of behaviors.

The competition of people's ideas and creations in the marketplace (and the most qualified applicants getting specific responsibilities) betters a society. But there is a difference between competition for social excellence (the less motivated or talented still have "enough") and competition for social dominance (winners gain such control over future winnings that people get left out).

It is normal for businesses with the same product or service to compete. People will naturally want to go where they get the best and this competition can maintain quality products and service. But ever-growing populations have resulted in huge for-profit corporations out-competing small businesses, controlling politics, and not paying their full social and environmental costs. They control a system that overrides the necessary cooperation for all to have basic needs for living – clean air, pure water, nutritious food, meaningful work, adequate housing, and equal opportunity for self-development. We can't have healthy, peaceful civilization without this fundamental cooperation.

Whether in the jungles, in urban streets, in corporate-led economies, or between ever-growing nations, it is my studied opinion that wherever cultures require competition for the above needs, they grow less and less civilized.

In any competition, including healthy, peaceful livelihood, if winners keep winning, it means losers keep losing. Nothing reduces the motivation to try like losing repeatedly (even while getting blamed for not trying). Only one person or team can gain the benefits of coming in first in competition, no matter how hard all the competitors try. By default, then, many losers are supporting the opportunities of fewer winners. Most adults living in poverty came from parents living in poverty. Their lot was already cast in their first years of life. Meritocracy largely disappears with overpopulation.

Competition gets many people addicted to an adrenaline rush. It makes us feel powerful, but we are not meant to be adrenaline junkies.

Scientists now know that which genes get turned on and which get switched off depends on what we experience and learn from our social and physical environments, especially when we are children and most especially in the first three to five years of life. That's when 90% of the organizing of our brain occurs (think mapping or hard-wiring). That sets the emotional and motivational stage for which future learning is easiest and which is more difficult (less likely to be learned). To avoid carrying on with uncivilized genes, we, obviously, need to grow and learn in a civilizing environment, one that promotes health and peace.

Scientists studying brain and body chemistry also know that we are happiest and live the longest given the following: when we mostly eat what our bodies were designed for, when we get daily exercise, when we are mostly in control of our own lives, when we are feeling loved by and loving others, when we are helping others out of kindness, when we have a sense of humor, when we can be ourselves and freely share those selves with others, when we feel part of and identify with a community, when we are relaxed and content more often than not, and when we live in a tranquil, natural (Nature's own) environment. These long-term health and peace benefits are difficult to regularly obtain or maintain in an ongoing atmosphere of urban crowds, competition, over-stress, oppression, or danger.

In our brain and body chemistry, the prevalence of oxytocin, endorphins, dopamine, and serotonin mean long-term health and peace. Adrenaline, norepinephrine, cytokine, and cortisol are internal chemicals secreted for dealing with stress and danger. They are meant to help us only temporarily. The default status of our nervous system is supposed to be mindfully at peace, not ever tense from anticipating and worrying about the next obstacle or problem because of competition from overpopulation.

Today, competition between people (not just their ideas and products) is reinforced in many ways.

Basically, competition determines who gets what when there are not enough resources or opportunities to go around. Competition arises in large families when there are too many children for the amount of available parental nurturing. Competition gets established in large classrooms where there are too many kids for teachers to give the individual attention each needs to thrive. Test scores, grades, and class standing become exclusion tools. Competition is necessary to determine who gets what opportunities (like getting into college) when there are too many young people for everyone to develop his or her unique potential. Getting employed these days is more like beating competition among many qualified candidates.

Two thirds of U.S. citizens follow competitive sports. Schools and colleges are better known for their athletic teams than their academic programs. Coaches are paid way more than professors. Jocks are more popular than nerds and the most violent sport gets the most attention. Our entertainment glorifies aggressive actions between people.

Our commercial media is hooked on reporting competitive sports like they are the most important events in life. They also find it easier and cheaper to report political news using sports terminology. We learn who's winning and who's losing and their strategies. (It's more exciting than explaining policies.)

Competition is the name of the game for successful businesses, though different for the banks that lend them money to beat competition. By law, bankers only need 10 or 20% of money they loan actually available. They just write the total figures into their accounts, declare "it" loaned to business heads and do the same for their competitors, lending money into existence to support competition. And all the while, the banks are collecting interest on the full loans until paid back in full – getting ever bigger and more powerful in the economy (like too big to fail).

Some people are deservedly well-off financially because of their creativity, but most rich, upper-class people got that way because they or someone in their family background were selfishly competitive.

I don't know about you or your family, but study after study confirms that most repeated winners of competition develop a sense of superiority and entitlement over non-winners. (Actually, you may have noticed in our competitive culture, the same tends to be true with about anyone having more power than those around them, whether the source of that power is height, muscles, attractiveness, guns, or money.) The same is true more often than not when their financial power is inherited. And, if they have "good" reason, people with power over others tend to ignore or exploit those others to one extent or another.

Study after study shows that repeated winners of competition and most wealthy, upper-class people, in general, have less empathy and compassion, are less concerned about justice, are more selfish, and are more likely to engage in and morally justify unethical behavior compared to people with not-rich, non-upper class backgrounds. My apologies to the exceptional, but these are the findings – as power and wealth increases, positive regard and interest in others below their financial standing decreases. (Even new big lottery winners tend to adapt to the passing pleasure of big purchases and lose sight of the happiness gained from the simple pleasures in human kindness and in Nature.)

These same studies confirm that people from lower class, non-wealthy backgrounds (again not all, but generally) have more emotional intelligence, display more empathy and compassion, show more interest in fairness, and are more generous, kind, and helpful than rich, upper-class people. (And we still want to live like which?)

Psychologists, Dacher Keltner and Paul Piff, are leading experts on scientific studies of greed and personality.

We hear about gambling addiction; wealth addiction is the same, except it grows ever easier to win.

To be sure, there are some wealthy people who are ethical and generous. But winning and power and wealth are highly addictive. Such addicts conduct their lives in ways that provide regular and growing "fixes." They become power-mongers. Overpopulated habitats for them are like taverns to an alcoholic. They need all those "underlings" to manipulate and control to get more fixes.

By 2012, the richest 20% in the U.S. owned around 90% of its wealth – that was not the case before Reaganomics took over (1980) followed by Clinton's free trade and globalization push and more Reaganomics by George W. Bush. It's been calculated (Oxfam) that just 1% of the world's population now have about as much wealth as the other 99%. In early 2016, just 53 men and 9 women had as much wealth as half of the world's population. How many billionaires are using their money mostly to help bring health and peace to the planet? How many are mostly like emperors keeping themselves and their empires growing ever more powerful and opulent. I say, in a democracy, any power over people that can't be voted in or out must be regulated.

In an overpopulated and thus competitive world, most wealthy and powerful people (feeling superior) like to think they earned their wealth and power by themselves. To them, luck or educational opportunities or public infrastructure or those who helped prepare the way or made it all safe, etc., had little to do with it. This justifies their belief that they are entitled to more privileges and resources for their lifestyles than those "below" them.

This also leaves more people to do without or compete for favors from the powerful (enough to satisfy) or fight each other for the "crumbs" that the powerful leave (some do so on garbage dumps). In overpopulated societies, for some to gain (and think they deserve it), others have to lose (and are supposed to think they deserve that too).

As populations keep growing, competition keeps growing and established "winners" get conservative about change.

The biggest winners of competition between people are usually the promoters of that competition. The captains of commerce are telling our kids they must study harder and do better (in the subject areas that big corporations need) so we can economically outcompete other nations in the future. They are not telling them to learn to become better thinkers for their community's health and peace. They are not telling them to study to become better citizens of democracy and better stewards of the planet. They are not telling them the future needs smaller families.

Competition as a way of life destroys the empathy and compassion needed for cooperation and collaboration. Men, in particular, have long been taught to numb their emotions (except anger) in order to be more competitive. Competition for living erodes the collective trust required for peaceful societies. Relationships become strategic (as in trying to gain something from or get ahead of somebody) instead of authentic (just being real). People don't get relationship needs met. Long-term goals of health and peace no longer guide short-term choices. Trying to beat the competition disconnects them. Social and environmental problems develop that don't get fixed. They become the new normal for the next generations and trend away from sustainability.

Too many children per socialization system (families, schools, communities) and too many people per natural habitat result in competition to get power over as many as you can (become bigger, stronger, faster, smarter) and hang on to that power. As overpopulation continues and more competition gets set up by the minority of winners and their groups, it becomes more selfish, unfair, and unethical. In democracies, they use their power to gain control of education, information, and communications to keep voters unaware and distracted. Government policies keep getting more conservative, even as more liberally knowledgeable people are alarmed at where we are headed.

Wealth equals power and power is not given up easily. Even in democracies, unchecked power leads to inequality and inequality to social deterioration.

Wealth-addicted people have always been threatened by majority rule. The non-rich majority can become envious and suspicious of the rich. They can vote to better regulate financial dealings. They can increase progressive income tax brackets and estate taxes, especially after overpopulation makes upward mobility all but impossible (as is now the case in the U.S.).

Democratic governments can make rules limiting the "fixes" of wealthy movers and shakers. They can cap interest rates, require truth in contracts and product labels, charge full payment of social or environmental costs for affluent lifestyles, and more. So, the wealthy like weak governments they can control. In hard times, the wealth-addicted provide the answer. Government is the enemy (the parts they do not control). If government bureaucrats would just get out of the way, people would be better off (said Reagan). And reducing taxes (especially theirs) will improve things. (It really means less government to mess things up for them.) Overpopulation actually leads to more government and taxes (for police, courts, prisons, and militaries) in unsustainable efforts to keep health and peace.

Overpopulation creates the biggest danger in a free society, that the highly competitive, wealth-addicted rich take advantage of that freedom and use their riches to gradually take over the culture. In particular, they hire their own politicians and buy up newspapers, television, and radio broadcasting media to get people thinking their way through falsehood and fear. They rig the system to maintain power, institute their values, teach the non-rich that they just need to keep trying to be more like them, and run that society's civilization into the ground. So goes the U.S. currently. (See the research of economist, Thomas Piketty.)

Even the Bible said it was easier for a camel to pass through a needle's eye than a rich man to get into heaven.

There seems to be three basic choices for our economies. (Any similarity to the "science" of economics is purely coincidental.)

1. The supply-side choice has been to keep increasing the population (potential customers) and the production of goods and services for them to buy. As net profits go to those supplying the capital, they are to increase production and innovation which is to increase jobs and standards of living for the increasing populations. While it quickly develops a mutually-benefitting local economy, ever expanding this economic system eventually makes it unhealthy and unsustainable for people and planet alike. It produces a hyper-competitive, selfish society with income inequality and fewer prospects for the next generations. It also leads to the exclusion choice.

2. The exclusion choice is cutting unqualified and moneyless people (losers in the competition) out of the prevailing economic pie and letting government (welfare) or religions (charity) take care of them. Calling them too stupid or lazy to work helps justify exclusion. Incarceration is popular if they turn to illicit drugs and crime. Aside from the immorality of this position (and revolting taxpayers), it is certainly not sustainable. Exclusion economics with growing populations eventually result in such numbers of excluded that they can no longer be controlled and all hell (mass killings, extortions, kidnappings, drug wars, terrorism, etc.) breaks loose.

3. The only sustainable choice is attending to the demand-side of economics. That is decreasing the demand for goods and services both by decreasing the numbers of people in need (or want) of them and by living simpler, more locally self-reliant lifestyles (quality not quantity) until both are in balance with the natural resources and opportunities for learning that can supply them indefinitely. This is a true resource-based economy.

Humans can only create and maintain civilization (truly civil) with lifestyles based on higher overriding values that unite all stakeholders. (That's individuals developing their unique selves in ways that contribute to the well-being of all society.)

These higher values are sustainable health and peace. Health and peace must include liberty and justice which includes equal opportunity and healthy environments. These values can unite us because they are in every human's DNA (and get expressed when born into the right social/environmental conditions). When population numbers exceed the carrying capacity of their habitats, power over other people becomes an overriding value. More power of some sort (bigger, faster, smarter, wealthier, or more shrewd, sneaky, corrupt, cruel, sociopathic, etc.) wins more access to resources, opportunities, privilege. Overpopulation gets us to "nice guys finish last." The competition divides stakeholders and their groups and thus results in ongoing conflict and social ills.

The U.S. once had a mainstream of cultural values portrayed in movies, television, songs, news sources, etc.) that kept us growing more united. Now, what we have are culture wars of growing confrontation and selfishness. Simply put, competition, in and between large families, large classrooms, large schools, large businesses, large cities, crowded habitats, and crowded nations has us learning attitudes and behaviors that are not conducive to health and peace. Furthermore, winners can use their winnings to keep winning and form powerful controlling organizations (empires). They look down on non-winners as deserving losers to intimidate and oppress. They feel entitled to more of Nature's bounty and use it to display their "superiority." The powerless tend to compete to do their bidding for rewards instead of uniting to challenge the system. Both winners who keep winning and losers who keep losing tend to become psychologically unhealthy, some even dangerous to the rest of society.

For competition between ideas and creations to work in a cooperative system geared for health and peace, a culture's population must be in balance with sustainable resources and equal opportunities to learn and work.

In right-sized populations, all children and adolescents can get equal educational opportunities and every adult can choose the "price" of his labor and products in local "free" markets. In right-sized populations, the more industrious and talented can still be rewarded with more money from the market-place. Meanwhile, the lesser capable (or motivated in different directions) will still have ample resources for their essential needs and opportunities to see where their potential development takes them. There would be no scarcity of resources or opportunities to enhance the value of money, possessions, or status beyond what's practical. Equal opportunity for all, plus democracy and a wise constitution of boundaries, would be consistent with sustainable health and peace.

With appreciation, admiration, and respect coming from social benefits, the more industrious and talented have a natural incentive to share any knowledge, expertise, material gain and wealth (the cooperative piece). This "socialism" is by bottom-up free-choice (not top-down legislation or edict). There is no incentive or reason for expanding market control or inflating the price to make undue profits.

Humans are basically the same as they were 10 and 20,000 years ago. They can only handle so much competition, or stimulation, or convenience without becoming less healthy or less human. When it comes to economic output, too strong, too fast, too big, too many, and too complex, can be as problematic as too weak, too slow, too little, too few, and too simple. Technology should enhance our humanity, not lessen it. Modern countries need to declare economic development largely "done" and seek a workable "steady state" economy. Earth's ecologies already have us in transition toward this whether we like it or not. The longer we ignore it, the poorer future generations will be when it is finally accepted.

A necessary ethic for civilization is "Love thy neighbor as thyself." In other words, behave in ways that convey positive regard for others' well-being. Anytime you've got it in you, give it freely, but it is not the bottom-line answer to maintaining sustainable civilization.

While empathy, compassion, and love are certainly necessary for a healthy, peaceful world, it is physiologically impossible to feel those feelings simultaneously with what we feel when we are under all the stress of today's competitive and complex lifestyles. We have to be sufficiently relaxed to genuinely feel empathy, compassion, and love. Otherwise, we are only going through the motions (insincere and wearying). Being in touch with loving feelings is not readily possible in our demand-filled, over-scheduled "rat race" cultures set up by the leaders of competing businesses and political empires. We lose our connectedness to each other. And the more overpopulated we get, the more chronically stressed and deprived of loved and loving feelings we become while trying to get ahead or stay ahead.

The resulting crazy fall-out, the anti-social ripple effect cannot be overestimated. Those with money (or credit cards) keep trying to buy happiness with ever more, bigger, faster things. They are slaves to fashion in clothes, housing, and the next big thing. They transport their bodies from place to place in expensive machines that are extensions of their personality. Dependent on technology, they carry and stare and poke at flat little boxes too much of the day and night for scant relationship needs. They also take astonishing amounts of pills for overstress, for anxiety, for depression (and get hooked on opioids).

However, the worst examples of love deprivation, in my opinion, are: finding it fun to perpetrate violence in computer games, enjoying savagery as entertainment in movies, carrying guns on our streets to feel powerful, deterring murder by killing those convicted of murder, and forever seeking peace by setting up the conditions for war.

To combat unethical and abusive competition, all the world's major religious traditions in the last 10,000 years developed a version of *The Golden Rule*. *The Golden Rule* sets the standard for cooperation and collaboration. "Do unto others as you would have them do unto you."

The title, *"The Golden Rule,"* gives these words a handle to make it easier to hang on to and hand off to others. However, *The Golden Rule* has been perverted by the competition and selfishness generated from overpopulation. It now fits reality as, "Do unto others before they do unto you – pass you, control you, block you, crowd you out, take you down, etc." For the super-rich (the 1%), *The Golden Rule* might be updated as, "Who has the gold, makes the rules."

I repeat! Too many winners of competition get addicted to feeling superior. (The United States has yet to get over World War II and that was a necessary war.) Such winners use their winnings to insure that they keep winning. They also like to display their superiority with selfish consumption of resources and by having their way with "losers." Losers are seen as inferior and deserving of their fate. (Many losers come to believe it.) How many have to sell part of their individuality to depend on winners for identity and/or paychecks? How many have to do their bidding just to survive?

Civilization falls apart when people are divided into a few greedy winners (haves) and many inferior losers (have-nots). Civilization fails when people are left out. Some of them rebel and sabotage civilization. In the extreme, established winners resort to "shock and awe" nuclear weapons to maintain the status quo; losers retaliate with "shock and awe" suicidal missions to upset it. Bye, bye, Golden Rule and health and peace. Hello, cruelty, suffering, and premature dying. The real problem is too many people.

The Golden Rule can no longer stand alone. It needs a back-up rule. For that I propose *The Legacy Rule*. *"To best love your children, create no more or no more than one or two."*

The Legacy Rule furthers the goal of all children growing in ever-increasing health and peace. It moves us toward enough clean water, adequate nutrition, and sufficient psychological nurturing for each and every child. *The Legacy Rule* makes more effective socialization and education possible. It gets us closer to adequate-paying work for everyone. It also means more opportunities for more maturing of individual potential. It gets us to the uniting values of cooperation and collaboration necessary for sharing habitats in health and peace.

The "why" of *The Legacy Rule* and the means to implement it need to be globally dispersed. This is far more important and effective than the trillions the world spends on its militaries. Only world-wide understanding of its importance, the universal use of contraception, and an ethic of family planning in keeping with *The Legacy Rule* will restore the uniting values that beget sustainable civilization.

This could be the first ending to this book.

Of course, the devil is in the details and I've added more pages to cover more details. One huge detail is this: once overpopulation of habitats set in and the quest for power over other people became necessary to secure needed resources, the physically weaker sex got pushed into the category of less important. They became second-class citizens or breeding stock for more workers (or more "cannon fodder"). Nurturing people became less valued than aggressive people. Testosterone became favored over estrogen (and young men have to prove they have more of it or get called "pussies"). **One of the first casualties of overpopulation was women losing equal standing and equal rights.**

The Legacy Rule will find little traction without the promotion and protection of the following rights for women.

1. A woman may or may not share some responsibility for making a man horny, but no woman ever has to share responsibility for relieving a man's horniness. A turned-on man can always masturbate. (In fact, masturbation plays an important role in getting to a sustainable civilization.)
2. Any woman has the right to say "No, thanks" or "Stop" or to change her mind at any time in sexual relating, sexual posturing, or sexual conduct and have that be respected, no matter what she's wearing or not wearing and no matter how far any sexual activity has progressed.
3. Neither sexual assault, nor rape, nor any physical violence against any woman is ever justified.
4. Marriage is not a prerequisite for sexual activity.
5. No woman should be forced into marriage or forced to stay in a marriage.
6. Every woman should have the freedom and the means to choose if and when to have a child and to stop after one or two.
7. Women have the right to be as healthy and educated and prosperous as men. The U.S. ranks 45th out of 144 nations in women's social, political, and economic parity with men. (Education for women is especially important for reducing overpopulation; they can fit into society in ways other than just motherhood.)

If men are to be men, they have a right to (appropriately) pursue women for sex. However, women are neither objects nor property. They have a right to refuse sex and to halt any pursuit they don't want. When women feel secure in these rights, they can be more receptive to sex and may pursue it as well (and display more beautiful sex appeal too – don't know about you, but I like it).

Another early casualty of overpopulation was racial and minority discrimination.

Can you imagine the bafflement and anguish of the welcoming natives of the under-populated Americas when the early explorers from overpopulated Europe first landed on their shores? With their competitive and greedy mentality, many of the early explorers and colonists were actually more like terrorists promoting genocide. And who called whom savages? Then, as Native Americans tried to defend their homelands and treaties were eventually made to keep peace, we know which side kept breaking them to make room for more immigrants arriving. Before long, many new European colonists also joined the world's slave trade, kidnapping Africans and selling/buying them like property, especially in the warmer South where they could work on cotton plantations.

Overpopulation of habitats regresses humanity. The resulting competition soon begets violence and war. Before technology made the difference, majorities naturally won the battles. People in bigger tribes and (later) bigger city-states and nation-states became the conquerors addicted to feeling superior and entitled; lives in smaller tribes and ethnic groups (minorities) mattered less. And discrimination to keep minorities at a disadvantage after getting control of them insures that they can't rebel against their oppressors.

Obvious physical and ethnic differences in the vanquished make discrimination easier to maintain, consciously and subconsciously. It gets imbedded in cultures long after the initial conquering. That disadvantaged peoples fail to develop themselves under disadvantaged conditions supposedly justifies keeping them disadvantaged. This racism, of course, still goes on today and grows where populations continue growing. (The U.S. has yet to get over the Civil War.) The underlying problem is too many people.

How about adding *The Legacy Rule* to any conversation about saving the environment?

Human infrastructure now covers half of the inhabitable areas of the planet. For our health and peace, natural beauty should surround us – not be something we drive to. It is a bad sign when a trail has to be marked "Nature" Trail.

With their explanations of complex social and environmental issues, it seems to me that representatives of organizations devoted to halting environmental destruction end up just "preaching to the choir." That appeals to and validates the already converted (also helps contributions).

Unfortunately, the majority of people outside "the choir" lack a readiness to hear (the same problem that more learned politicians have with more thoughtful speeches). It doesn't connect much with the typical overstressed and disempowered-feeling person in the workplace worried about paying the bills. It connects even less if unemployed and/or living in poverty. (Political and religious extremists with faulty, but simple answers can do better.) The typical person today has more pressing problems or agendas than to relate to complex explanations about why we need to change our lifestyles, the same lifestyles they may be trying to hang onto or get into.

In addition to their reporting why we need to moderate or change our habits of consumption, I suggest all environmental organizations publicize *The Legacy Rule* at every opportunity, while explaining how it relates to their cause. Otherwise, they are "ignoring the elephant in the room." They would be giving quick, uncomplicated counsel that has a better chance of being remembered and considered. At the least, repetition would keep the message spreading in public conversation.

In fact, in explanations, the average person might want to hear how having fewer children now makes a family financially better able to improve their life. And having fewer children is the number one long-term accomplishment anyone can do for the environment.

I say we all need to be publicizing *The Legacy Rule* and doing so repeatedly.

Research says, on average, only 10% to 20% of what we see and hear is remembered for any length of time if we don't immediately involve ourselves with it in some way. Research also shows most of us only attend to news and information that already fits our biases. This argues for reminders, something more than whatever sex education or sexual counseling we get. Repeated "nudges," especially after a thorough explanation, can result in more people changing. *The Golden Rule* took centuries to become more universally known. With today's digital technology, *The Legacy Rule* could become known practically everywhere in weeks. This message can be easily, inexpensively publicized repeatedly all over the world ending: using every available media. It is hoped that various people with more moxie and connections (and digital expertise) than I can join this mission and get it rippling ever outward.

If we can spread cell phones everywhere, we can spread contraceptives everywhere. But frequent reminders of *The Legacy Rule* in the world's electronic and print media will more widely accelerate and maintain discussion and understanding about the necessity of their use. The basic idea is to keep it in the world's consciousness as much as possible.

I have to conclude that living by *The Legacy Rule* from now onward is the most important action any individual can do for improving future civilization (and to insure our survival as a species). We need to be shouting it out like a sinking ship shouts "Mayday!"

The Legacy Rule needs to be crossing everyone's mind, at least, as often as the urge to have sex. (It won't, but it should.)

Population management is an issue of ethics and morality (the glue of civilization).

Unfortunately, every day's total of new additions to the world's population means more global warming, more environmental deterioration, more forests disappearing, more species going extinct. (Earth is not one big shopping mall for which you only need money.)

More children increase the future competition for acquiring the essential needs for health and peace. Less children increase the future cooperation for acquiring the needs for health and peace. One approach generates more money and power and privilege for the current "winners" of competition. The other generates more money, power, and privilege eventually for everyone.

One direction holds winners as superior beings having more value and losers as inferior beings having less value and that each deserves to be where they are. This makes it okay for the superior beings to treat the inferior beings as lesser humans. This increases all sorts of evils.

The other direction holds that all people deserve equal opportunities to develop their individual potential and discover what of their unique strengths contribute to society. This results in more locally diverse ideas, creations, and innovations to share for building, maintaining, and enjoying a sustainable quality of civilized life. Autonomy, mastery, and meaningful use of one's developed skillset are the major ingredients of individual happiness.

In much of the U.S. and the Western world, the top 10 to 20% of income "earners" have little idea what life is like for the rest. Wealthy capitalists now own most of the means of production for what people need and want. They are set in centralized monopolies taking in most of the money generated by the working and creating majority. While anyone can be creative and entrepreneurial in the digital age, the problem is making a decent living in the competition controlled by plutocrats. Plus, overpopulation requires urbanization. That erases more self-reliant options.

We have made many valuable technological advances in trying to exist with overpopulation, but they won't save us.

Some of them have to do with getting more food and nutrition out of water and soil. First, there was agriculture itself and then irrigation. Later came industrial farming with ever more sophisticated equipment. Most important have been the developments of artificial fertilizer manufacturing, the Green Revolution in grain and rice production, and now genetic modification of food crops.

The laws of Nature say we can't get something for nothing. More technology requires mining more raw materials and dumping more waste. Not all that much of the Earth is meant to be a mine or a dump.

The use of technologies for living with overpopulation is too much like treating the symptoms while ignoring the cause. Improvements will be temporary. The basic problem is too many people per carrying capacity of natural habitats. In fact, the technologies mentioned above resulted in a faster rate of population increase after being made available. In a generation or two their users became worse off because of all the more mouths to feed and more competition for land, water, and fertilizer to do it with. (The people of India and the Philippines are good examples of this.)

Without a doubt, our brilliant engineering technology has made more lives healthier longer, also more stimulating, more convenient, and more fun. And engineers can maybe make food in laboratories and probably improve on recycling and reusing technology's waste and disposal. But coming up with an equitable, peaceful system for determining who gets the benefits and who doesn't because of the impossible numbers of people needing/wanting them may be the bigger problem.

Other technologies that won't save us either.

Desalination (taking salt out of ocean water) can be done on a small scale, but not large enough to solve our water shortages. This technology requires much energy and severely pollutes the ocean and/or land around it (with salt, duh).

Sinking deep wells into the huge aquifers of near-fresh water newly discovered under the ocean's continental shelves is a better way to buy us more time, but . . . most fresh water is needed for growing food. With either desalination or deep coastal wells (or towing icebergs), moving the new water away from the coast to the fields where most food is grown is so energy intensive as to make these technologies super-expensive. Nature designed Earth to have water ever moving from land masses toward the oceans. How long can we oppose Nature (same as God) on such a large scale? (Nature is the same as God in my book – I'd expect repercussions.)

Nuclear power is said to give us "clean" energy that gets us away from burning dirty fossil fuels. Unfortunately, safe nuclear power is an oxymoron. Any technological process that produces waste by default so dangerous for so many for so long should simply not be done. We really need to speed up the pace of improving and using solar power, wave generation, and maybe local geothermal units for our energy needs – also battery storage.

Many people believe that we can develop the technology to colonize other earth-like planets in outer space. (It makes interesting movies, but there is no Planet B.) And if we found one, mathematics says there is no way we could ship out excess people fast enough or soon enough. We are Earthlings. We don't have sufficient resources for the necessary transportation and adaptation. (Only the elite could afford to go and who would they get to do their sweat-work?)

More technology is not the answer.

Much technology today first seduces, then handcuffs us into life-styles of accommodation that serve big corporations, but don't really better our humanity. Our minds are being hi-jacked – we are losing autonomy of attention. It also liquidates resources ever faster to make more money for corporate investors. There is no logical reason to believe that we can keep coming up with technological developments that would permanently take care of ever-growing populations of humans on not-growing planet Earth.

It's not just a question of engineering the technology. It's also being able to afford the energy costs, the land loss, the pollution, and, most of all, the deteriorating quality of life as living becomes ever more complex and unnatural. We came from Nature. We are designed to be creatures of Nature.

Individuals and small families and scattered villages of them can have their way with Nature without disrupting ecosystems in any significant way. They can build cottages to live in and clear land for gardens, fields, and pastures to produce food without lasting harm to Nature's design (if the soil is organically cared for).

On the other hand, big, dense urban concentrations of people living in hugely equipped houses and apartment buildings with con-crete streets and parking lots and motor vehicle traffic and malls of stores and skyscrapers of offices kill off large portions of Nature. And the fallout doesn't stop there. Keeping all these people sup-plied with water, food, sanitation, medicine, and stimulation in the absence of Nature has all sorts of harmful ramifications, especially when the energy required comes from fossil fuels. How many of these mega-cities can Earth afford? How long can we oppose Nature (same as God) on such a large scale?

A finite planet with finite resources for human living requires a finite population of humans living in balance with those resources. (Nature's laws are the Higher Power.)

The technologies that can save us are already developed.

They are long-acting reversible contraceptives (LARCs), particularly modern IUDs and small matchstick size, under-skin implants; either one prevents pregnancy for years. We also have "morning-after" pills that prevent a fertilized egg from becoming a pregnancy if passion gets ahead of the unprepared. In addition, we have up-to-date distribution technology that can make contraception fully available and modern communication technology that speeds up socialization, education, and information relating to their use. These are the technologies we have to work with – already working, but needing more attention and distribution.

Injectable contraception that lasts for months is now available. It can be easily and discreetly administered by health workers in regions where women want contraception – and more control over their own bodies. There are also new promising sperm-sterilizing techniques currently being tested for males. They do not affect libido and are reversible. Then males can better share responsibility for moving in the direction of appropriately-sized populations. Most importantly, when coupled with complete sex education, these technologies can give family planning choices to all people, freeing them for increasingly healthy, peaceful living.

If we want to use science and technology to decrease premature death rates (as in civilization) then we also have to use science and technology to decrease birth rates. We can't have sustainable civilization otherwise.

It is surely a natural right for every adult human who wants to have a child to do so. Creating babies enhances our humanity. The question is how many babies. It is not an issue of pro-life vs. anti-life. It is an issue of which anti-life position is best. Creating new human life should not take priority over meeting the health and peace needs of existing human life and that includes newly created babies. Meeting the needs of existing life does no harm to imagined and possible life that stays nonexistent.

So, when will U.S. political leadership fully address the over-population problem here?

Our two major political parties are best summed up as follows: Not enough Democrats get it and too many Republicans get it wrong. Both parties are infused with an empire-building, perpetually growing mentality.

Both parties are dedicated to the following economic system. Ever-growing populations mean more spending-customers buying more goods and services. This means more profits for investors to create more business expansion. This means more jobs for more people to become spending-customers buying more goods and services and so around we go in an ever expanding circle, making everybody ever better off. More recently, construction (more jobs) plays a big role, building ever more and bigger houses and apartments and strip malls for more shoppers to spend more paychecks to furnish them. This is a population growth-driven economy; it cannot continue indefinitely.

When the circle slows down (a recession), Democrats try to help the workers and consumers become better able to work and spend. Republicans try to help the financiers and investors to expand business activity. On average, this economic circle has been getting slower for some time. Since 1980, the financiers and investors have been getting most of the political favors and tax breaks. Consequently, the rich have gotten wildly richer, but wages and salaries for about everyone else working have stagnated. Meanwhile, the population keeps growing. Unemployment and underemployment are now rampant. More and more people are unable to enter the work force and more and more people are being left behind. This drags the system further down (welfare, ill health, crime, law enforcement, prisons, etc.). The real problem is too many people, which neither political party will look at.

Our economic system has put us in a double bind and there is no quick fix. We have made economic development an end in itself (greed) instead of a means to an end (quality living).

Currently, two thirds of our economy (U.S.) depends on consumers buying goods and services. Most ecologists say we must shrink consumer-driven economies; most economists say we must expand them. For their livelihood, most people now have to rely on ever growing populations buying more products and services. (And no politician wants to be responsible for ruining the economy.) But Earth's habitats are finite. Their life-giving resources are not increasing. They can only absorb so much waste. Our economy is consuming its base and we can only use so many things and conveniences in our lives without harming our bodies and limiting our minds in the first place. We can only grow so much economy without ruining our planetary home and debilitating ourselves in the bargain.

We got on the road to a better life without an exit strategy and then overshot sustainability. Now we've got to back up and go with "stagflation" until we level off with sustainability. (Our Federal Reserve economic leaders quake at the thought.) No doubt about it, the necessary changes will cause much confusion, chaos, and upheaval, some of it deliberately perpetrated by people financially and psychologically well invested in the status quo. One way or another, changes will happen and they will get more stressful and scary regardless.

Either we tackle the side of the double bind we have more control over or wait for Nature to cull our species' numbers, which will prompt acting out the worst of our own sub-human nature as we go down.

Either we each and collectively change our numbers and impact on the planet as humanely as we can in the shortest possible time, or Nature will continue making changes for us with her wind storms, floods, and droughts, with resulting thirst, hunger, and opportunistic diseases, and until robbing and killing each other for basic needs becomes an epidemic across the globe.

Seek to understand ourselves and others and only judge consequences. Guilt and defensiveness rob us of energy to grow
and change. *The Legacy Rule* is always meant to start from
this point forward.

Know that our free-will, our freedom to choose the best course of
action, is always limited to our previous learning opportunities.
Know that all people, individually and collectively, at any moment
in time, possess a specific fund of available knowledge, a particular
measure of physical ability, and a certain amount of will-power (self-
discipline or self-control) to act. This was true for every human being
at every moment in the past. If they and we had had more knowledge
or more ability or more will-power, we all could have done better with
the values of health and peace (it's in our DNA). But we didn't and
so we could do no more than we did. Thus, we all did the best we
could up to this point in time (right now) toward making a healthy,
peaceful world. Realizing this advances the values of compassion and
forgiveness toward people, yourself and myself included.

It is also true that from any given point forward (from right
now), each and every one of us has the potential to do better
toward making a healthy, peaceful world than we have up to this
point in time. That is, we can if we get and take or make the right
opportunities to further learn more relevant knowledge, and/or
enhance our physical abilities, and/or develop more will-power.

Knowing this advances the values of community support for
liberal education (dictionary definition), ongoing public information, a variety of real experiences, life-long learning, and rehabili-
tation from wrong-doing. We need growing free-will for growing
self-reliance. It requires growing in knowledge, in abilities, and
in self-control. From today forward (every today), we can acquire
more of this power to accomplish more daily steps in the direction
of furthering health and peace. (And "think globally, act locally"
is good advice.)

We must look to the findings of social, behavioral, and life scientists to develop a sustainable cultural and economic system.

To live on Earth in health and peace, we have to engage reality. Science does it best. Authorities are not experts in reality simply by virtue of their position of power.

Science refers to methods of discovering knowledge that are least affected by the biases (psychological filters) of the seekers and investigators. Every one of us, including any scientist, will interpret new experiences according to past learning background, memories, and present emotional status. This can contaminate our understanding of present reality. To counteract this tendency, scientists set up investigations of reality in ways that can be duplicated by other scientists with different biases. These ways include documenting and recording details and measurements and designing strategies for isolating and controlling variables. When other scientists with different psychological filters follow the same procedures and get the same results or come to the same conclusions, possible knowledge is discovered. They also publish and present their research and findings for peer review (so more biases can weigh in).

True science is a process that never settles on a final answer. It never claims to 100% prove anything. Its questions are always open to further investigation. This makes science self-correcting over time. Earlier wrong conclusions are just part of the learning process. Science continually seeks to disprove its findings and accepts as knowledge of reality only what it cannot seem to disprove.

Science is not a special interest group or ideology. Evidence and logic from science should never be discarded for matters of belief. Methods of science have yielded knowledge so spectacular as to enable humans to walk on the moon. They have also been used to show how humans can live sustainably in maximum health and peace on planet Earth, but enough people have to learn about, be willing and able to change, and implement this knowledge to make it so.

All Nature exists as a whole, universal system of relationships.

Every sub-system is related to every other sub-system and every part of every sub-system can change or vary. Every variable affects other variables. Each is a cause and a reaction. Nothing is independent. Every change-event affects other events (some measureable, some not – yet).

When a system is like a ball or a sphere, there are no roots or every point can be seen as a root because all other points lead away from it. Planet Earth is a biosphere hurtling around our sun with a terrarium of life held on by gravity. If its human life is to be sustainable, its families, its economies, its cultures and lifestyles must fit together harmoniously with its ecologies.

This interdependent reality does not fit our tendency to have our complex institutions of business and government made up of specialists, particularly specialists in engineering or business administration. Even our scientists have to specialize, though consulting different disciplines is becoming more common. Maybe the worst outcome has been the majority of economists with no knowledge of ecology – taking us on this grand experiment with greed.

Alexander von Humboldt was a Prussian scientist who first saw Nature as a system that humans should value and protect. He warned us over 200 years ago that human industrial activities could change the climate. Dr. James Hanson, a NASA scientist at the time, first warned the U.S. Congress about global warming in 1988. To our peril, in 2016, we still had voters, members of congress, and presidential candidates that think it's a hoax. (OMG! We just elected one of them.)

All people need some understanding about the interdependence of the whole natural system and how their area of specialization relates to it (and other sub-systems within it). Most leaders in government and business are still too narrowly educated and experienced for that role.

It still serves understanding to talk about roots.

The more significant players in Nature's community of life are not human. They are decomposers (bugs, worms, etc.) who depend on nutrients from carnivores (meat eaters) who depend on nutrients from herbivores (plant eaters) who depend on nutrients from plants who depend on nutrients from the decomposers and around it goes in a cycle of interdependence. Humans evolved to depend on every part of this cycle for their sustenance. (Too many are woefully ignorant of this – they keep poisoning the decomposers, killing off the carnivores, and destroying the habitats of all.)

To keep going (as in sustainable), this major cycle of life also requires some fundamental supporting components, namely sunlight, clean water, healthy soil, and mostly moderate temperatures. In our ignorance, while trying to live with overpopulation, humans have impacted both the major players and the fundamental supports in ways that are not good for life, especially higher evolved life.

By sheer numbers and power, humans have become the biggest (short-term) change-agents in Nature's system. From the vantage point of human activity, then, it is still useful to talk about roots, the roots of civilization and the root causes of deteriorating civilization. I call the latter "evils" because they, directly or indirectly, deliberately or subconsciously, cause harm, suffering, and premature death among humans.

Willfully causing preventable suffering is causing evil. Human-caused evils include oppression, violence, rape, murder, torture, terrorism, warfare, using weapons of mass destruction, suicide bombing, ethnic cleansing, and genocide. Human-caused evils also include poisoning, polluting, and destroying our natural habitats when it harms humans. Committing evil is not from our highest nature and evil is not sustainable for humans on planet Earth. To stop evil from recycling, we have to go after its roots. Evil must be checked or, sooner or later, all humanity will be.

Isn't money the root of all evil?

The pursuit and accumulation of money certainly causes a lot of blindness, deafness, and fuzzy thinking. In the U.S., money now determines what's in the air we breathe, the water we drink, and much of the food we eat. Money dictates what news, information, and education we get – not really adequate for voters in a democratic-republic. Friends and family, health and freedom, all take a back seat to the pursuit of money. The bulk of most everyone's adult life in the developed world is organized around getting money incoming regularly. Still, I don't think it's very useful to call its pursuit the root of all evil or not needing money the root of all civilization.

Money symbolizes a debt to be paid or a promise to be fulfilled with something of worth. By itself, it has no value. You can't drink it, eat it, or take shelter under it. If there is no water or food or shelter, money is useless. Money buys long-term happiness to the extent that it prevents or solves problems. But it is meant to merely be a convenience in civilization.

In overpopulated societies, money symbolizes power. When people must pursue money for the power to have a decent life, it's a sign of too many people for Nature's bounty. That Nature's bounty is carved into pieces by certain people who got there first and/or "won" the right to sell it off for more profit than needed (more power) is also a sign of overpopulation. Overpopulation puts value on power to get ahead of others. That's behind money obsession and wealth addiction and growing inequality of its distribution. Wealth-addicted capitalists use their money to buy more power. In the U.S., they take over local, state, and federal governments, pay the lowest tax rates, and change regulations for even more power. It is most definitely not the key to sustainable civilization.

The roots of all willful human-caused evil (preventable suffering).

After 50-plus years of studying human beings and their dysfunctional societies, it is my judgment that we need to consider three roots of evil – and their opposites as the basic directions toward sustainable health and peace.

I think it is most useful to declare the first root of all evil to be insufficient knowledge and faulty beliefs about Nature and human nature and their relationships. (I view Nature and God as the same concept.)

Among all the consequences of insufficient knowledge and faulty beliefs about Nature and human nature, is the second root of all evil. We reproduced our species to overshoot the carrying capacities of our natural human habitats. There are too many of us for all to live in health and peace.

This consequence gives rise to the third root of all evil: the quest for power over other people. It now plays out as empire-builders organizing followers into hierarchies of power in order to outcompete (get power over) the lesser organized, minority groups, and the unorganized to secure needed resources when there aren't enough to go around. The first empires were military and political, but, eventually religious organizations and big businesses followed.

Empire-building results in leaders getting addicted to power and entitlement, followers remaining dependent in thinking and doing, and the powerless being exploited and having their homelands plundered. From the in-power empires' perspective, it's too easy to categorize non-members as expendable and competing empires as enemies.

By using their power over others (the third evil), leaders of empires like to control education and information to favor their leadership (perpetuating the first evil) and forbid sex education and contraception to expand their empires through larger families (promoting the second evil). All evils can be traced directly or indirectly to the above three roots. They are the bottom-line reasons for our less-than-mature humanity (see page 116). They are the downfall of sustainable civilization.

The first root of sustainably healthy, peaceful civilization is universal knowledge of what makes it so. Spreading this knowledge is the number one cultural commitment every society needs to make.

When we can mature to our potential, human beings are not evil by nature. All people need to be receiving basic education and ongoing information geared to the requirements of mature functioning in sustainable civilization. It must be as objective as possible – that's free from empire-building influences (like political ideology, corporate propaganda, or religious indoctrination). This knowledge must be gleaned from the ecological, biological, behavioral, and social sciences. (Methods of science come closest to objectivity.) I fervently believe this education and information needs to be focused on the following fundamental areas above all:

1. How to take care of one's self physically and psychologically AND (most importantly) how to do it without significantly interfering with numbers 2, 3, 4, and 5 as follows.
2. How to get along with other people.
3. How to be a responsible citizen in a democratic republic.
4. How to live ecologically on planet Earth.
5. How to be effective parents, teachers, mentors, and good examples to the next generation (can't have sustainability without it).

In priority, these broad learning goals have to become "The Common Core," ahead of and embedded or infused within language arts, humanities, mathematics, physical sciences, engineering, computer science, and business administration. This is the knowledge that enables people to best govern themselves (local self-reliance – not empire-reliance). We will only get sustainable health and peace everywhere in the world when people everywhere know how to make it and keep it locally so themselves. (An economy based on the myth of perpetual abundance doesn't do it. Learning how to serve empires trying to outcompete in that economy really kills it.)

The second root of sustainably healthy, peaceful civilization is human population numbers in balance with the carrying capacities of natural human habitats. Attaining this balance is the number two cultural commitment every society needs to make.

Carrying capacity means health and peace resources sustainably available for all (includes each new generation). Carrying capacity also includes equal opportunities to learn. The key to sustainable civilization is scientifically-determined population numbers stabilized at the indefinite life-carrying capacities of natural human habitats. For healthy livelihood and psychological maturity, the numbers of humans have to be and remain in balance with the resources for living and the opportunities for learning how to sustainably make use of them.

The situation of "too many people" negatively impacts and limits individual learning of all five of the behavioral requirements (lifestyle components) previously listed as necessary for universal health and peace. This negatively affects health and peace in adjacent areas and eventually all areas of the world. (Check the latest news about refugees.)

We are not just human beings. We are sexual human beings. Life is sexually transmitted. Our adult bodies want to regularly have sex. This is in our DNA. (Celibacy is not.) Young adults, with their testosterone and oxytocin levels, have to be more than human or less than human to make abstinence work as birth control, especially if masturbation is also held to be wrong. The less-than-human option will include lots of male competitive aggression. Empire-builders like young competitive aggression (some give 'em guns and bombs).

No one is born willfully lazy, stupid, ignorant, violent, or a "loser." When they don't have to compete with each other for needs and opportunities, virtually all people can readily learn and live the necessary uniting values for health and peace while developing their individual potential within those boundaries. This is our common bond – in our DNA – no competition, conflict, or war can actually kill it (only cover it up).

In keeping with *The Legacy Rule*, all organizations working for health and peace should be spreading sex education around the globe, including the need for birth spacing and family planning, and the means for contraception.

To have this be a part of every culture is in the best interests of everyone, but especially younger and future generations. No sex education or sex counseling will be complete without covering knowledge about the future social burden of large families, the benefits of small families (with adoption as an option), and the differences between overpopulated habitats and appropriately-sized habitat populations. Many differences (benefits) we can't begin to grasp until we get there – we never before in our history had right-sized populations coupled with vast information and entertainment technology available to everyone. Right-sized populations have also never been paired with our miracle-working medical technology (though far less would be needed) and modern non-polluting transportation for everyone to appreciate.

The use of the Internet can be a tremendous help in spreading sex education and family planning information. Videos can cover examples of contraception and demonstrations of their use.

The spread of television in general and soap operas specifically designed to illustrate the benefits of small families are credited with the swiftest, most dramatic lowering of birth rates in many overpopulated countries. Television can be a window to different worlds and different possibilities, especially for women. Seeing is believing and female emancipation from a lifetime of motherhood tends to follow.

Research actually shows childless couples and couples with one child to be happiest in today's world. (Much of the world, including the U.S., has been growing less family friendly for most couples – too stressful and too expensive.)

I do not think abortion should be part of any population reduction or stabilization policy.

The abortion issue requires less emotional reaction and more reasonable discernment. Even embryologists (scientists studying embryos) cannot tell when human life actually begins. And part of the growing mass of cells after an egg is fertilized is developing placenta. The female body does not naturally change to signal pregnancy until after implantation of a fertilized egg in the uterus one to three weeks later. Over a typical married woman's reproductive lifetime, when not using birth control, many fertilized eggs avoid implantation and pass out of her body naturally. Are they human babies lost?

In my view, the most useful (and natural) determiner of when human life starts and stops is when the human heart starts and stops (naturally). The heartbeat is the first movement after three weeks or so of actual (implanted) pregnancy. In the 4 to 6 weeks before heartbeat, I think terminating the cell build-up is nobody's business but the woman involved. However, after the heart is beating, maybe that tiny life should be called a human baby and given some legal consideration while in its womb-home. This would also clarify other prenatal issues.

That said, real life does not often come with just two clear choices, one good and one bad. Later abortion may still be the least unfavorable option given the mother's health status or in special cases of incest or rape. There is also the possibility of sufficiently obvious faulty development of a fetus so as to condemn it to endless suffering if allowed to "live." (Consider the Zika virus and microcephaly.)

For abortion decisions after a fetal heartbeat has started, maybe the mother, her physician, and a judge will be best, not one-size-fits-all edicts from higher-up religious leaders or governments. We should not lose sight that universal sex education, readily available contraception, readily available morning-after pills, and public family-planning clinics are the best preventers of abortion.

Population research for sustainability.

Exactly what numbers of humans any nation's human habitats can carry sustainably depend primarily on the amount of fresh water, suitable food-growing soil, and temperature ranges available. Secondarily, right-sized numbers depend on the quantity and complexity of possessions its citizens collectively think are necessary and the resources required to manufacture, distribute, maintain, and eventually dispose of them. (Consider more natural environments vs. more artificial environments, stimulation and entertainment from real humans and Nature vs. digital and virtual stimulation and entertainment, personal automobiles vs. mass transit, locally grown food vs. mass produced and shipped in from afar, human and solar energy vs. fossil fuels and nuclear, throw away vs. recycle, wasteful fads and fashions vs. conservation of raw materials, etc.)

We have plenty of research data to compare the health, happiness, and peacefulness in nations who have the most consumption of resources per population density with those that have considerably less of either. That makes the United States one of the most over-populated nations on Earth. The data says it is also one of the unhappier, less healthy, and lesser peaceful nations on Earth (compare gun ownership and gun-shot statistics with other developed nations).

Scandinavian countries are closest to right-sized population numbers. They were the first to require age-appropriate sex education in public schools. And they are able to offer free medical care and free college education (or nearly so) to all. Using standard measures of civilization, they are considered to be among the happiest, healthiest, and most peaceful nations on the planet. (They do still have problems to work out to get to a sustainable economic model – and maybe need a still smaller population.)

Your legacy needs to include this rule:
Create no more kids or one or two.

Check out the following assertions online.

The nations of the world with the most conflicts tend to be the most overpopulated. Nations being flooded with desperate immigrants from other overpopulated areas are also more conflict prone. One underlying cause is certain religious leaders keeping women uneducated and in child-bearing roles to enlarge their empires. While nothing in the Quran prohibits the use of contraception, most Islamic nations in the Middle East and Africa are crowded beyond their resources and opportunities (a tradition of several wives bearing children for each rich-enough man doesn't help). Extremist groups like Al Qaeda, the Taliban, Boco Haram, and ISIS or ISIL have no problem finding recruits with nothing to lose. The Philippines and many Central/South American countries with a tradition of Vatican Catholicism long dominating their governments have too many people for health and peace.

The Overpopulation Index ranks countries according to the sustainability of their current population. Some 77 nations are currently consuming beyond their environmental means and must secure resources from elsewhere, now or later, whether elsewhere likes it or not. By this index, the top 15 overpopulated nations are Singapore, Israel, Kuwait, South Korea, Jordan, United Arab Emirates, Japan, Lebanon, Iraq, Belgium, Italy, Netherlands, Switzerland, Egypt, and Spain.

China was once a worst case, but a much criticized urban one-child rule has improved their plight and will continue to pay off through every next generation. Thailand was blessed with a special economist, Mechai Viravaidya, who used novel ways (worth imitating) to get that country's birth rate reversed in just 15 years. Iran was once headed for crushing poverty. Their leaders did the most effective (and socially acceptable) reversal of population growth of any country. It turned their situation around in one generation. Compare that to Pakistan or Nigeria or the U.S.A. (Unfortunately, the profiteers of overpopulation often generate a backlash to undo these efforts.)

The population numbers we need to get to.

Most computer work by population scientists (ecological and agricultural demographers) currently indicates we have about twice as many people for sustainability in the United States and, maybe two or three times what our planet as a whole can support indefinitely. What that could mean for our grandchildren is not easy to think about.

If it had been miraculously possible for all newly family-starting couples to follow a one-child policy beginning in 2014, we would have gotten the world's population down to around two billion by the end of this century. Some of the first population scientists maintain that two to three billion is the ideal world population size to stabilize for maximum sustainable health and peace everywhere on planet Earth. Still other scientists with up-to-date measurements (from *Population Matters*) say we could sustainably make do with as many as five billion people. (That still puts us two billion over and climbing.)

Two billion or five billion? Whether we humans just want to get by or have more natural quality of life in our sustainability is also part of the issue. More population reduction allows us to actively regenerate the carrying capacities of depleted human habitats to get more people out of poverty. And we can increase more forests and grasslands to pull more carbon back out of the air and sequester it back in the earth (where fossil fuels come from and should now stay).

What we know for sure is that nearly all nations in the world need to be reducing their populations, most especially India, China, Nigeria, and the United States. Incompatible economic, religious, or political traditions need to change no matter how chaotic the transition period. (The alternative will be worse and eventually not survivable.)

Every present and future child needs every present and future parent to follow and promote *The Legacy Rule: To best love your children, create no more or no more than one or two.* This is the legacy all children deserve.

What about the age-old argument that we need enough younger generation numbers to support and care for the numbers of elderly.

I believe that when parents fully understand what's at stake (complete sex education), most of them will not wish to procreate enough young to make sure one or more will provide for them in their elder years. Government Social Security income is the civilized way to go, but from a risk pool treated as income insurance on a need basis.

In the U.S., wealthy-enough elders do not need youngers paying payroll taxes on their behalf. And the cap on earnings paid into the fund means workers pay a higher percentage in taxes than the wealthy getting capital gains and interest. That cap needed to be done away with a long time ago. Other modern countries spend about 10% of GDP on their elderly and disabled. The U.S. spends around 5%.

Also, people who learn how to physically and psychologically take care of themselves in their youth will more likely have more health and independence in their older years before passing. Less people make this education more possible. These healthier elders can help provide care for any dependent and frail elders in their communities with new healthier elders always "arriving" as the former age. Smaller families mean less over-stressed younger parents who will have more energy to look in on their aging parents and/or for volunteering to help care for frail elders as well in community homes.

Digital equipment, automation, and robots (also trained animals) are assisting more and more with elders, although, hopefully, never to take the place of human caring.

Other considerations for care of the aged.

Funds saved by having fewer children and young people to educate and regulate and make sure they are provided for (as in welfare safety nets), plus fewer criminals resulting for law enforcement, courts, and prisons to spend money on; these monies can be diverted to help care for frail elderly. Even with fewer children growing up, there is still likely to be a problem providing full employment with all the corporate automation, computer software, and AI robotics planned for the future. Employment in elder care would be an option.

Audits of the military spending in the U.S. and around the world ($1.5 trillion in 2013 alone according to the data firm, HIS Inc.) would show a monstrously obscene amount of unnecessary spending. I think it could be better used to improve education (including sex education) and basic infrastructure (including family planning clinics) to really secure sustainable health and peace. And there would be plenty left over for elder care.

I also believe physician-assisted, peaceful dying at home should be an available choice for a person to freely make who is terminally ill or permanently bed-ridden. (Check out Switzerland's position on this, also the Netherlands.)

Countries such as Japan, Poland, South Korea, Italy, Taiwan, Cuba, Germany, and Spain are already "top-heavy" with more older non-workers than younger workers. They are in position to lead the way. How they manage can show other nations what to do (and not do) regarding elderly care with fewer young people.

One thing is sure; the transition period of more elders than youngers to a stabilized equal number of both would be temporary.

Civilization means living better than animals.

Because we are sexual beings by nature, we require family planning to not reproduce like animals (and then fight and starve like animals when our habitats are full).

Nature does not tolerate overbreeding – or overly changing the habitat of any one species because of overbreeding. She requires balance between their numbers and their ecological niche of life supports. Any species that thinks they can conquer or ignore Nature will be purged. Nature is the Higher Power.

However you define modern civilization, a certain range of population is necessary to achieve it and to keep it sustainable in any habitat. Beyond that means too many people for health needs and requirements for peaceful living. The worst is the lack of emotional intelligence competition brings to society. (Real men don't cry – or recognize others hurting.) With a wall around your feelings of empathy, compassion, fear, sadness, hurt, etc. you'll be a tougher competitor (and maybe get to be boss). We need to be asking ourselves, "What kind of life do we want our children, grandchildren, and great grandchildren to have?"

If you track them back far enough, virtually all the problems of living in health and peace that you experience, observe, and read or hear about would be helped by less people. Directly or indirectly, they are all symptoms of a malady called overpopulation. This is true if for no other reasons than we get more effective socialization with smaller families, more effective classroom education with smaller class-sizes, and more incentives for civil behavior with smaller (more relationship cohesive) communities and neighborhoods.

The automatic improvements to any part of the Earth when all citizens knowledgeably (unselfishly) pursue the intent of *The Legacy Rule* are astounding. The following (partial) list is what having world-wide social norms of truly responsible sexual activity can accomplish sooner or later.

Less people on planet Earth will decrease or eliminate:

- Hunger, starvation, and poverty.
- Lack of safe drinking water, lack of hygiene and sanitation.
- Contagious and degenerative diseases.
- Overcrowded classrooms, schools, and colleges.
- Relationship problems and child-rearing problems due to over-stress, lack of parenting education, and lack of time.
- Drug abuse, addiction problems and other problems stemming from overstress, anxiety, and depression.
- Bankruptcies, foreclosures, unemployment, low wages, slave labor, homelessness, welfare need.
- Oppression, injustice, crime, drug trafficking, gang warfare, domestic and social violence, rape, kidnapping, child abuse and neglect.
- Forced prostitution, trafficking in sex, sexually transmitted diseases.
- Racism, castes, classism, sexism, paternalism, chauvinism, misogyny, hate crimes, all manner of prejudice and discrimination in housing, employment, and lending practices.
- Economies skewed to favor the rich, corporate welfare, a shrinking middle-class, a growing gap between rich and non-rich.
- Sidewalk, mass transit, and traffic congestion, also traffic accidents, resulting medical costs, and fatalities.
- Mining, drilling, and development in pristine wilderness areas and "loving national parks to death."
- The growing world business of smuggling (exploiting) migrants and refugees.

Less people on planet Earth will decrease or eliminate:

- Inflation: the rising cost of anything affected by ever increasing demand and ever decreasing raw materials, the rising cost of medical care, prescription drugs, energy, tuition at colleges, rent, family homes, transportation, etc., etc., etc.
- Ever growing costs (taxes) of maintaining and providing more infrastructure to accommodate ever increasing populations in cities, also roads, bridges, electrical grids.
- All manner of ecological disruption and environmental degradation, including polluted air, water, and soil, ozone depletion, acid rain, also soil erosion, contaminated wells, aquifers going dry, landfills overflowing.
- Livestock confinement, algae blooms, collapsing fisheries, oil spills, wet-land destruction, tree diseases and over-cutting of forests, mudslides, desertification of grasslands, loss of farmland to development, loss of pollinators, noise and light pollution, the "tragedy of the commons."
- Habitat destruction, poaching, and species extinction – most with still unknown medicinal and other chemical, genetic, and ecological values.
- Global warming causing extreme heat, longer droughts, fire storms, increasingly powerful wind, rain, and snow storms, ocean acidification, dying coral reefs, rising ocean levels from melting ice sheets, greater flooding of lowlands, along with environmental refugees and all the expense of coping, rebuilding, resettling. This is becoming the most life-threatening consequence of too many people living too affluently with energy powered by fossil fuels, while the rest want to keep the option open so they can dream of getting there too.

Less people on planet Earth will decrease or eliminate:

- Misinformation, disinformation, fraud, corruption, competing ideologies based on fear or obsolete tradition instead of real data and evidence.
- Lack of courtesy or manners, lack of respect, lack of trust, living in fear and paranoia, doublespeak, computer trolling, hacking, and viruses, stereotyping, profiling, political polarization, lack of uniting values and ideals.
- High taxes for inefficient top-down, big-brother or nanny government with one-size-fits-all regulations creating local problems where they don't fit.
- Data collection of personal lives by government and/or corporations. Selling and misusing that data.
- Dictatorships, totalitarianism, plutocracy, oligarchy, theocracy, erosion of and lack of democracy.
- The rise of extremist left-wing guerrilla groups or right-wing violent radicals that seek to take over societies by any means and never compromise or give up.
- The taxpayer's expense of supporting enough police, courts, and prisons to preserve order, and the monstrous expense of developing arms and maintaining militaries for "defense" (or fighting for more resources).
- Nationalism, ethnic conflict, child soldiers, terrorism, war, refugees, genocide, the threat of human annihilation from weapons of mass destruction, including biological and chemical warfare and newly developed smaller nuclear weapons whose use is more "thinkable."
- The threat of extinction of the human species on planet Earth.

Family planning with modern contraception for one or two children (one is good – two is enough) conveys more future benefits to more people at less cost than any other available technology.

Everyone in the entire world should be learning why this is so. In the U.S., that's not what the people we elected have been spending much of our tax money on. We continued to increase our Pentagon budget when we should have reduced it considerably after the breakup of the Soviet Union. We continued developing "shock and awe" weapons when we should have been increasing domestic and foreign aid, especially for education. What we have done to our college students in the last two decades (saddling them with huge debt) is obscene. (And less than 1% of our current federal budget goes for non-military foreign aid.) We have been limiting sex education and defunding family planning clinics when we should have been substantially increasing both. We have been lowering taxes when we should have been raising them (progressively) to pay for past military build-ups and wars, government entitlements, corporate subsidies, and environmental damage. We have been deregulating big for-profit corporations when we should have tightened regulations, especially to protect the environment and maintain decent-paying employment and contain the cost of medical care. And we have automated and robotized factory jobs plus shipped them out of the country for cheaper labor at the same time that we opened the gates to immigration and encouraged more population growth at home.

Promoting and adhering to *The Legacy Rule* is the people's way of solving the above long list of social and environmental problems – what our ever growth-minded, empire-building leaders in politics, business, and organized religion cannot accomplish sustainably.

The Legacy Rule as political power.

Growing overpopulation transfers power away from individuals and communities to ever bigger, higher, more complex organizations. There is one thing that having less people will not do. It will not make today's wealth, privilege, and power-addicted empire-builders more wealthy, privileged, and powerful. Thus, plenty of empire heads will find fault with the idea of even stabilizing population growth. They are fighting and will continue to fight population reduction by spreading fear of change and "bribing" plenty of followers to their cause.

Empires, whether political, corporate, religious, or otherwise cannot exist without a constant supply of up-and-coming young people who, thanks to overpopulation, have fewer options in life other than giving their support with their labor, paychecks, "product" loyalty, worship, or even life itself (dying from unhealthy work, combat soldiering, suicide bombing). So, the structure of empires always has the many making possible the power and wealth and privilege of the few. This is only possible because overpopulation limits free-thinking and freedom of choice.

There is a difference between cultures of mostly young people working for mostly better-off older people and then eventually succeeding them generation after generation versus cultures of mostly non-rich people and their descendants working for rich people and their descendants throughout their lives generation after generation. The latter cultures grow out of the competition and empire-building and greed that get established with overpopulation.

We must stop providing power-mongering empire-builders with excess numbers of future young adults actually competing to be used by them for their psychological and financial addictions and agendas. Remember, the biggest winners of competition are usually the promoters.

Right off, the world's supply of working-age people needs to shrink. That's the only real solution to poverty and its multitude of consequences.

Most people today need full-time work and decent income (not part-time or called-in-on-demand jobs) in order to live in health and peace. Instead, employment continues to be eliminated by computer software and robotic technology, also out-sourcing and off-shoring while big investors get wealthier (more bubble-up than trickle-down).

The number of new job-openings among the world's employers today is no way close to the number of young people entering the work force today. Unemployment and underemployment are now chronic problems in about every "developed" country and more job-erasing technology is on the way. How much artificial "intelligence" do we need?

With qualified applicants per job-opening always increasing, the amount paid those newly hired decreases relative to inflation. Profit-minded employers can always get somebody else if the hired complains (while CEOs' salaries and compensation are obscene). The percentage of corporate profits going to workers has been decreasing for decades. We now have so many applicants per job-opening, that employers automatically reject anyone not already employed. What are they supposed to do?

Instead of workers competing for available employment we need to have employment competing for available workers. Profits for owners and investors will go down with higher labor costs, but a decreasing labor pool means more people will find work and better paychecks. In spite of some jobs lost and some prices increasing, when the power between employers and employees balances out all workers will be better off and owners will still be okay or have other options. There will also be more opportunities for start-ups as big businesses, dependent on growth, shrink or collapse.

One of the many rippling impacts of new births today.

Unfortunately, new births increase the future competition to find decent-paying work for paychecks to buy essentials for living. At this writing there are something like seventy million young people in the world who are unemployed and the number is growing by half a million per year.

The governments of some countries are trying to take up the slack, either by employing people to build useful infrastructure (best way to buy time), providing make-work jobs, putting them in their militaries, or just giving welfare to the unemployed and underpaid. This is better than nothing, but it is also unsustainable and taxpayers are revolting all over. (Some are more revolting than others.)

Currently, some 15 to 20% of young people in the U.S. are not able to find work or go to school; it's 33% to 50% the first two years after high school (depending on race). They can't live off parents while occupying themselves with computer games and social media (and/or drugs) forever. Suicide is a leading cause of death among the young. A few become so deranged living in this limbo, they commit mass murder before killing themselves, just to prove that they mattered (with plenty of guns to so do).

More "ambitious" young people, without appropriate opportunities, form or join gangs with their own economies based on drug and sex trafficking, protection rackets, extortion, bribery, kidnapping, etc. They may also have to get into wars to protect their operating turf from other encroaching gangs. (Currently worst = Mexico and Central America.)

The left-out and disempowered are also ripe for joining fascist groups who give them status and cause to oppose ineffective or corrupt governments and established order with the power of political/religious ideology and guns and bombs. (Currently worst = Middle East and West Africa.)

The issue of immigration.

Immigration is a world issue because nations successful with their population policies will strongly attract people from unsuccessful nations. Immigration becomes contentious when it adds to the overpopulation of a host country. (Too many people in a lifeboat will take them all down.) And the most difficult part of the immigration issue is being able to discuss it without being accused of racism. There can be a difference between being opposed to an immigration policy that increases overpopulation and being opposed to people who are immigrants.

The reality in the United States and many other nations is that corporate empire-builders lobby for open immigration because it means more customers for their products and services and less labor costs to produce them. (The more applicants per job opening, the less an employer has to pay.) The United States allows much more immigration than any other country, at this writing about one million legal immigrants per year. Nearly 15% of people currently living in the U.S. are foreign born.

Abundant immigration guarantees social/ethnic conflict as immigrants will be perceived as taking jobs and pay-raises away from natives in the host country, as well as raising taxes for settlement costs, even when not. It does not help that most people prefer to live in communities in which they have the most in common, especially if they are new immigrants. So, multi-cultural societies do not mix much until their children's or grandchildren's generation. (And that depends on schools and community racist attitudes.)

We also have a political party (Democrats) whose leaders know it will get more votes with more immigrants becoming citizens. New oath-taking citizens are more likely to keep up with what government is doing and, rightly or wrongly, Democrats try to do more for everybody. (The other party, these days, mostly ends up just helping the rich.)

The best immigration policies.

Like anyone, immigrants should be treated fairly and their courage respected (even illegal immigrants). People migrating from one country to another bring with them new, different ways of thinking and living. Ordinarily, this can invigorate and improve the host country with new cultural ideas to consider and enjoy. Unfortunately, in overpopulated countries it polarizes more than invigorates. ("Far Right" politics get invigorated.)

I see granting temporary asylum to refugees fleeing danger or homelessness as a different (humane) matter than immigration to become new citizens. Otherwise, until more nations take responsibility for reducing their own population to carrying capacity, I believe it is best if immigration into any country is matched in numbers by emigration out of that country. It is also best if who gets to come in is decided by lottery and families are kept intact. New immigrants need to be knowledgeable about and committed to the intent of *The Legacy Rule*. Forgive my bluntness, but it makes no sense for new arrivals to keep the same breeding habits that made their previous home country overpopulated. Integration goes best if immigrants can speak or are taught the prevailing language of their new country (no need to give up their own) as well as demonstrate agreement with secular democracy.

What we want to get to with depopulating the world down to sustainable levels is open borders everywhere for cultural exchange, recreational and educational travel, and citizen diplomacy. Swapping residences and/or employment with people in other countries, temporarily or even permanently when mutually agreeable, would be immensely desirable and valuable as well.

This could be the second ending of this book.

Unfortunately, empire-builders, with their competitive, bigger is better mentality, fight depopulation every step of the way. More about that follows.

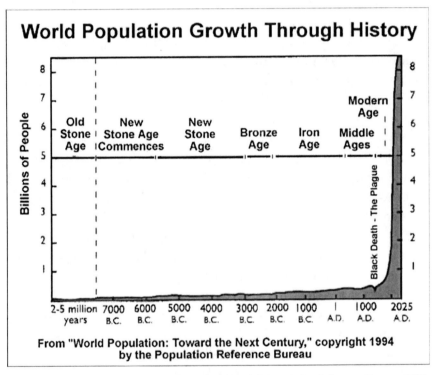

World Population Growth Through History

Billions of People

Old Stone Age | New Stone Age Commences | New Stone Age | Bronze Age | Iron Age | Middle Ages | Modern Age

Black Death - The Plague

2-5 million years | 7000 B.C. | 6000 B.C. | 5000 B.C. | 4000 B.C. | 3000 B.C. | 2000 B.C. | 1000 B.C. | 1000 A.D. | 2025 A.D.

From "World Population: Toward the Next Century," copyright 1994
by the Population Reference Bureau

Source: Washington, DC: Population Reference Bureau, 1994.

"The greatest county, the richest country, is not that which has the most capitalists, monopolists, immense grabbings, vast fortunes, with its sad, sad soil of extreme, degrading, damning poverty, but the land in which . . . wealth does not show such contrasts high and low, where all men have enough – a modest living – and no man is made possessor beyond the sane and beautiful necessities."

Walt Whitman
1819 - 1892

Not Sustainable

Not Sustainable

Not Sustainable

Not Sustainable

How overpopulation helped civilization (at first).

Overpopulation of the usual human habitats first stimulated the domestication of animals and the planting of food crops to supplement and eventually replace most hunting and gathering (except in rivers, lakes, and oceans). Especially by 10,000 B.C., with farmers able to feed more children to adulthood, the population really exploded.

Finding suitable, unclaimed land for growing food then became the problem. Excess numbers of young people without land for subsistence farming hung out in settlements which grew into small towns and got local economies started. Townsfolk needed food. They started making goods and crafts to trade for it. Farmers surrounding the towns could produce and trade surplus food for town goods and crafts that made their lives better. Young people in towns also perfected their talents to provide entertainment.

Townspeople introduced currency and opened shops, stores, and theaters (also taverns and brothels). Each group got money from their sales to buy what the other was selling. The lives of both town and country people were enriched and civilization, especially arts and crafts, and, eventually, education and science flourished.

Note: While this started several thousand years ago, in many rightly-populated areas, this beneficial relationship between rural and small town residents continues to this day. This was the case when I was growing up in Madison County, Nebraska, U.S.A. (minus the brothels). Everybody had an occupation of some sort – there were no homeless or hungry – and we never locked our houses or our cars – and sick neighbors always got help from well neighbors – and the local physician made house calls – and nobody ever murdered anybody – being sheriff was a boring job except during blizzards.

Overpopulation and the emerging of empires.

Still, town and rural interdependence enabled even more children getting born and living to adulthood. By 7500 B.C., various towns had grown into bigger cities and urban expansion continues to present times. Life, crowded into earlier big cities, was horrendously full of crime and filth and contagious diseases (many newly evolved). These conditions would periodically wipe out many city inhabitants. A prescription of early physicians for ill people was, "Move to the country." (Research says that's still good preventive medicine today.)

Cities are "high maintenance." As they grew ever larger, securing needed food, supplies, and building-materials, grew ever more challenging. Surrounding lands got to be insufficient for support and adjacent cities had the same problems. Aggressive leaders organized armies to fight for more territory while defending their own. Human history entered the age of empires competing to rule the weaker and unorganized. Basically, winning groups gained power and authority over subjects, made them insecure and fearful in various ways, and then provided the remedy of aid and protection if they stayed loyal and worked for the empire.

Eventually, winning empires controlled as much land as they could militarily keep and the conquered became slaves to work it. At one point in history, three-fourths of the world's people were slaves to empires. In less obvious forms, more slave labor continues today, including sex trafficking, forced marriage, debt bondage, military servitude, wage theft, and paychecks insufficient for living without welfare or charity. Empires also indoctrinate members as slaves to dogma and propaganda (no liberal/free-thinking permitted) to maintain their loyalty.

When people have not the resources or opportunities to maintain themselves in local economies, they must subordinate themselves (like slaves) to empire-builders who may provide some measure of secure life – a consequence of too many people.

Before they began an Arms Race, empire-builders started The Population Race.

As I define it, the major difference between empires and other organizations is that the leaders of empires continually try to expand their organizations. They need the power fix that comes with keeping their empire growing physically, financially, and/or dominantly with their members' help or coercion (or victimization).

Organizations tend to become empires when they must compete with each other for the same goals (like not enough resources or opportunities for their followers). Before money and technology determined their strength, leaders of empires had to concern themselves with manpower. "If we can get more members, then our clan, tribe, ethnic group, religion, city, state, nation, or whatever, can better defend ourselves against other such groups trying to get our land and resources." So, leaders expanded their following by providing incentives for large families of children, keeping women in life-long mothering roles, and prohibiting sex education and contraception. In time, this would have them running out of their own resources, but, if more members, their leaders could dominate or conquer (and tax) adjacent clans, tribes, ethnic groups, religions, cities, states, nations, or whatever, to get more (and get cheaper labor in the bargain). A modern version of the population race is that the "intelligent well-off" should have more children to offset all the children the "ignorant poor" are having. (How about better education?)

In recent times, political leaders, business leaders, and various religious leaders are still encouraging large families decades after science has established the need for populations to be reduced. Like any power, the power in having a bigger population under your control than the next competing organization is difficult to give up. ("You go first!") In my view, power-mongering is the third root of all evil.

Empires are organized in a top-down, military-like structure (best for controlling or conquering).

Leaders of competing empires know they can be more formidable by arranging followers in hierarchies of power according to their decision-making importance and abilities. Who tells whom what to think and do starts with the overall leader at the top (king, queen, general, commander, CEO, president, premier, pope, etc.) in control of the entire organization. It continues downward, usually with a board or cabinet of advisors, then officers responsible for whole divisions followed by managers under them ruling subordinate bosses in charge of workers at the bottom. The actual number of levels of power, as shown in a flow-chart, varies with the size of the organization and the mission.

The top-down power structure of an empire enables it to function like a military machine, to make decisions and move quickly against enemies or competitors. This is most efficient for securing scarce resources and opportunities as well as defending against competing empires seeking the same. Top-down powered organizations do best at getting their way with people (can also do best in emergencies). Bottom-up power (as in democratic republics) does best for health and peace.

Each level of power and each member within that level have assigned duties to perform that come from the top. What a higher-up says goes for those below. Those below are to be limited in their own thinking and actions. They have to be sufficiently under control for the success of the mission. Having them dress alike and do the same rituals and routines helps them think and act alike for easier control. So does a conservative education, passing standard (memory) tests, and keeping them uninformed about alternatives or misinformed about opposition and would-be enemies. All of this applies in hierarchically powered (top-down) organizations, military, government, political, business, religious or whatever.

Historically, empires integrated three major functions.

They are: (1) military and police-backed top-level leadership for control and administration, (2) the acquisition of property, supplies, money, etc. for the leaders and enough for the useful followers to remain loyal, and (3) the ministering of religious clergy to redirect the energies of the misfits and left-outs to work for a different reward – eternal bliss in the after-life. (Plus, leaders of empires always want God on their side.)

In modern times, these three functions evolved into more separate, but still symbiotic empire-building institutions. In the U.S., they have resurged in power in the 1980s as we became overpopulated and elected a Far Right president to lead us like an empire again. Military spending soared, big corporations were deregulated, and evangelical religious influences were imbedded into government. At this writing, top-down government in sympathy with huge corporate industries and pandering to we-know-we're-right religions are still powerful players in U.S. culture. Too much ownership of private enterprise has been divorced from community and Nature. Capitalism became more centralized and brought us to economic colonialism. We are all supposed to be competitive money-grubbing, spending, consuming subjects.

Unfortunately, public institutions responsible for education and higher learning, ecological and social research, environmental protection, for investigative journalism and public reporting, these were more and more defunded and sidelined. In the U.S., the power of an informed citizenry has been severely compromised by empire-building corporations marketing news that people want to hear in order to increase market share and sell more corporate advertising. Too many unqualified legislators are elected by too many uninformed or misinformed voters because of insufficient public education and information systems.

Societies function best when power is shared by all stakeholders.

As an adult, it is normal, natural, and healthy to want the power to control your own life (self-reliance). It is also normal, natural, and healthy to use appropriate power to control children's lives before they mature enough to control their own (adulthood). Having/using power to control other mature adults is not normal, natural, or healthy for either. Such power corrupts and positions of such power attract the corruptible. They also attract dependent followers who've had fewer learning opportunities for autonomy.

People who feel they have little control or are losing control over their lives are attracted to religions (and religious leaders) with the most powerful definitions of God. They are also attracted to powerful-sounding politicians (like Donald Trump) and "strong-man" rulers with big militaries on their side. (In the U.S., they are also attracted to guns.)

The best check on power is to keep it lawfully spread (shared) as evenly as possible among citizens, their groups, and their nations. Overpopulation kills the possibility. Then we get balance-of-power strategies between competing individuals, groups, and nations that escalate in ways dangerous to universal health and peace.

We can match the negative energy of others with more negative energy of our own. We can fight insults with bigger insults and hate with more hate. If we get bad treatment, or violence, or torture, we can fire back with nastier treatment, violence, or torture. We can be sure to have every new military weapon any other nation has, but more of them. We can go to war with more powerful explosives causing more destruction to keep on top of the balance of power. And, we can make sure our population is bigger so as to have more people to resist – or be left standing when the killing stops. This last strategy is the most insidious – everybody loses, especially the innocent next generations. The real reason for all such "wrong" balance of power efforts is too many people to begin with.

Some best ways to balance power.

Democracy and transparency balance the power between leaders and those being led in government, civic, and religious organizations. Unionized labor participating with management and ownership in corporate decision-making balances power between them. Cameras on police uniforms and cars balance the power with citizens being stopped and questioned. Progressive taxes and estate taxes keep the rich from getting so powerful as to buy their own legislators and government policies. Anonymous evaluations of supervisors and bosses, done by their subordinates and made public, balance the power in military-type and corporate organizations – wherever leadership power is top-down.

Educational opportunities should not depend on one's zip code or the wealth of one's parents or one's nationality. Universal, secular, equal public educational opportunities plus ability to stay informed are basic for balancing the power of citizens. They can then develop their own potential within boundaries that allow others the same rights. This degree of individuality also makes for a diversity of people that is practically uncontrollable by would-be empire-builders addicted to power. Our common DNA can still keep us united and cooperating toward goals of health and peace – when we don't have to compete for power over one another.

In the absence of right-sized populations for the above, would-be empire-builders use unfounded fear to recruit followers. (Fear is the favored way to control people – make them afraid of alternative ways of thinking, doing, being – and start when they are young.) In conditions of overpopulation, the uniting and cooperating only happen within organized groups competing or fighting others for resources. This causes losing groups to have less when there aren't enough. And sometimes "not enough" is determined by empire-builders and followers hooked on power and the greedy consumption that displays their "superiority." In any case, there's less health and peace for everyone.

Smart power for influencing other nations.

Smart power is not about "shock and awe" nuclear weapons or "shock and awe" paradise-bound suicide bombers. Compared to military power, smart power doesn't make private corporate contractors much quick money. It's just far more long-run effective at influencing hearts and minds in other cultures.

Smart power is modeling and promoting the values and lifestyles and government functions that other people in other nations would want to imitate. Smart power is offering citizens in other nations the best ideas from health and peace research, also direct aid for educational opportunities and information systems, contraception and family planning, and infrastructure for improving quality of life. How much of this got done in Iraq or Afghanistan during and after our long wars there? Contrast that with what we did in Japan and West Germany after World War II and compare the results. The Middle East is a powder keg that's not getting defused. It simply has too many people given the available resources and opportunities for everyone to have a decent life. That gets them "strong-man" leaders fighting war after war which only thins the population from the killing and fleeing.

Smart power is our greatest asset and the U.S. still has some government agencies (with meager budgets) and many non-government organizations spreading it around the world. Much more effort is needed, especially regarding science-based health and peace education.

Unfortunately, corporate empire-building interests have co-opted much of our government's foreign policy to favor them. They keep a media barrage of fear going to get citizens behind get-tough posturing and policies which help them get more government military contracts (and keep more foreign nations insecure and defensive). They even write trade pacts, in secret, including the right of corporations to sue governments whose regulations they don't like. (Their profits should be the highest priority?)

Because of overpopulation, the many are still making the few (empire-builders) more rich and powerful in order to try to live with trickle-down benefits.

We still have empire-builders competing to control people (now with digital monitoring, aggregate data collection, camera surveillance, and drone technology). We still have empire-builders promoting an arms race, a population race, a technology race, a liquidation of resources race, and a misinformation and disinformation race.

The U.S. version is mostly controlled by huge private, for-profit corporate conglomerates who also own enough "news" broadcasting and publishing media to keep any political candidates they don't like on the defensive. Corporate empires also now have the clout to form lobbying organizations (like ALEC) which ordinary citizens can't compete with. And they can now use their campaign contributions to, essentially, hire their own legislators. These corporate empires now have unlimited funding for negative political ads to mislead and scare citizens against any opposition. (Thank five current corporate-hugging, activist "justices" of the U.S. Supreme Court who see corporations as people deserving the same rights.)

In the United States, we still build and maintain massive militaries to protect the status quo and globally expand corporate interests. All those aircraft carriers and bombers and submarines (the enforcers of our Cold War empire) are real effective against cells of terrorists hidden in crowded populations of civilians??? (Religious sexual repression, lack of more liberal education, and not enough good jobs are the major factors behind young people becoming terrorists – they are left out of main stream living and alienated from government authority.)

A society or a world of competing empires cannot unite in pursuing and living the necessary values for sustainable civilization. Competing empires would not be necessary if appropriately-sized populations of people living in balance with sustainable resources were the norm.

It goes without saying, we certainly need organizations of people.

Organizations of people are valuable and necessary to modern civilization. Organizations of people can coordinate their efforts and accomplish goals of benefit to all that individuals acting alone cannot. They can build bridges and mass transit systems, manufacture back-saving equipment, develop computers holding and retrieving a world of knowledge and information, make medicines and contraceptives, operate hospitals and schools of higher learning, form communication networks, bring help and restore order after natural disasters, give aid to those in need, help keep the peace, etc., etc., etc.

Voluntarily joining an organization because you like working there as an employee or you just want to help with its mission is far different than being loyal to an empire. People who belong to an empire are generally (1) born into it and that's all they know for their identity and/or (2) they have to support it to feel secure and/or (3) they have no other choice for obtaining essential needs or paychecks to survive. The difference can well affect individual health, freedom, and development of potential.

In any times of emergency and crises, organizations with top-down rule by experts are most effective. But we do not need their leaders getting hooked on power, creating empires by perpetuating faulty beliefs, needlessly expanding membership numbers, and monopolizing resources for self-serving gain.

The best organizational structures for the mission of maintaining sustainable health and peace are democratic-republics (bottom-up in power) with educated and informed citizens considered to be the first level of government – governing themselves according to values in common. This requires right-sized populations who are well educated and don't have to compete with each other to live decently.

Real democratic republics are the opposite of empires.

For well-educated and informed people practicing mostly self-reliance in communities right-sized for their natural habitats, the most health and peace will be had in democratic republics.

In this form of government, the ultimate power is at the bottom; citizens learn to govern themselves in healthy, peaceful ways. They also vote on representatives to higher decision-making bodies with power, by law, to deal with problems bigger than any governing level below can solve. (This is the republican part of our democratic government.)

Unlike empires, democracies require time for ideas to be articulated and deliberated at the bottom levels of government, proposals negotiated and publicized, votes taken, policies implemented, consequences researched, etc. This can be a disadvantage in emergencies and crises (practically ongoing in conditions of overpopulation) Then an expert at the top giving orders to those below is much quicker.

Unlike followers of empires, truly democratic nations have the most freedom for their citizens to develop their unique selves. However, if we are to live in health and peace with other people in our habitats, no freedom can be completely free. There has to be boundaries to not encroach on other's freedoms. (Encroachment defines overpopulation – the more people, the less freedom.) As mature adults, we have to take responsibility to govern ourselves in this regard.

Because the United States was mostly settled by immigrants with mentality from overpopulated nations, many took to empire-building even in the midst of plenty.

(Wealth-addiction also migrated to the "land of the free.")

Other major differences between democratic citizens' organizations and empires.

1. I repeat! Top-down hierarchies of power (as in empires) invite abuse of power. Treated as superior, leaders begin to see themselves as superior and get addicted to those feelings. In the competing conditions of overpopulation, unelected leaders who manipulated, bullied, or out-fought others to get their positions of power have their success as proof of their superiority. Such toxic leadership (bad for health, morale, and the mission) is a common problem in our "modern" militaries, private corporations, and top-down religious organizations. Leaders and followers in winning empires believe that whatever benefits they win in competition are deserved by virtue of the superiority their group proved to possess. They develop a sense of entitlement over the less powerful and the "losers."

2. Empires have to grow their power to gain more benefits. Greater privileges, adulation, and monetary rewards provide the "fixes" for addictions to power throughout the hierarchy. However, like other addictions, it requires an ever more powerful fix to get the same "hit" over time. So the mission becomes continual expansion, preferably in ways that give leaders (their organization) a competitive advantage. Underlings get used for power fixes. People outside the organization become targets for power fixes. Power fixes get less and less ethical and more and more harmful. That spreads to inflict all of society. Other groups in competition for the same goals have no chance of winning something unless they also get more unethical and harmful to remain competitive.

3. Empires practice exclusion. One of the ways power-mongering leaders get their superiority addiction fixes is by deciding who gets what benefits and who does not, who has the right stuff and who doesn't measure up, who expresses sufficient loyalty or not, who exhibits enough enthusiasm and who is shirking. In political and religious empires, the more independent-minded, the questioners, and the rebellious may have to be made examples of, shunned, or expelled. Some religious empire leaders decide who's saved and who's damned. Corporate empires fire employees at will and set the price of their products such that only those with enough money can buy, no matter how essential. (All of this especially fits conditions of overpopulation.) Empires also support private schools and colleges which, by definition, practice exclusion. That promotes elitism and social classes which foster social discrimination and empire loyalty.

4. Assigned roles in the hierarchy cause members of empires to become specialists. This narrows their minds and their expertise to what their position demands. (It prevents liberalism.) Specialists tend to be conservative in any way that would threaten their status. This is part of the strength of the organization. It makes it difficult to change the course of an empire from the inside or the outside, even if the course is taking us all down (as in unsustainable).

5. Be they military, political, business, religious, or whatever, once leaders and followers get established as successful empires, their mission inevitably includes preserving themselves in the status quo and dominating, weakening, or destroying existing and potential competition. This hinders the development of new ideas and alternative practices and all but stops progress in building quality civilization. In conditions of overpopulation, it also leads to resistance and conflict from rivals for the same goals, which easily turns into uncivilized actions, even violence, terrorism, and war.

6. A most dangerous difference between democratic organizations and most government, corporate, and religious empires is that participants and followers of empire become dependent on whatever the empire provides. The usual scenario when corporate empires are powerful enough (often with political help) is to seduce, scare, coerce, or force people from their family farms, family businesses, and local economies. (It's been happening all over the world.) This kills their independence and self-reliance. Now they have to move to a big city, join the labor force and maybe depend on corporate empires, or on welfare from government, or possibly a religious empire for consolation and/or charity. That the newly displaced might be able to get hired for paychecks to buy things does not usually make up the long-term difference. Without much control over their lives, the stress, and the unnatural environment, their health and personal development are negatively affected.

The relationships dependents have within and toward controlling empires are too much like parent-child connections (being told what to think and do) which adults need to grow out of to mature. Adult to adult relating and adult functioning (physical and psychological self-reliance) is compromised in favor of the empire as determined by parent-like leaders. Participants and followers must sacrifice their individual development. They no longer have much freedom to grow in their own unique potential.

Mature adults do not automatically do as they are told and, consequently, don't fit into empires very well. Empire-builders like to start indoctrinating their ideologies into children for that reason. With prescriptions and restrictions, coercions and incentives, conforming rituals and dress, they can be made to think alike and act alike for easier control. Children can be made to psychologically stay somewhat like children and reliably depend on the empire and its leaders for what it is providing or selling, especially true of religious organizations who know God as "Father."

Leaders and supporters of empires are now the primary obstacles to a sustainably civilized world of maximum health and peace.

Because they exist to out-compete other empires, if any one leader adopts an unethical practice which gives them a competitive advantage, other competitors have to do the same to remain competitive. Some examples are ignoring how much they pollute or not paying a living wage or moving their money to offshore bank accounts or their headquarters to another country to avoid taxes.

Indeed, for leaders and followers to allow their particular military, political, corporate, or religious empire to get smaller or weaker is to invite other competing empires to move into the power vacuum and possibly be marginalized, exploited, oppressed, enslaved, or destroyed by them. Justifying and protecting their existence is the first duty of empires. I repeat! Power is not given up easily, even when dysfunctional to goals like health and peace. ("You go first!")

In the U.S. these days, big corporations are the foremost power players. If a social problem cannot be solved by private corporations making more profits, it probably won't get solved. Most corporate conglomerates cannot seem to stay in business with ethics and decency as their guide – exploitation and deception are built into their business models. Mistakes at the top affect the entire organization. Extortion or corruption somewhere in management will often be necessary to get results (rather than lose their jobs and not make their big-house payments).

Empire heads and their followers will likely continue to come up with unscrupulous strategies and tactics to maintain their power as long as we have too many people unable to ignore them and go their own way. The worst "going backward" problem today is people obeying fundamentalist empire ideology that abuses our liberal freedoms to gain more control and restrict freedom for others. (Support more "dictionary liberal" education.)

Government as referee.

If a half dozen neighborhood kids divide themselves into two teams and play basketball for fun, they can probably get along without a referee. In any competition, however, where the stakes are money, status, and privilege there had better be a referee or the fudging of rules will escalate. What one competitor does, others have to do to stay competitive which starts a race to the ethical bottom. In a competitive economy, government has to be rule-maker and referee.

In rural areas and small enough towns, little refereeing is needed between local competing businesses. Their owners will likely care about their reputations, their neighbors, and their communities. In the case of large cities and outside-controlled corporations, government has to be an effective referee. Most large corporation owners (stockholders) live outside the communities affected by their company's decisions. Most are likely to only care about profits and fire managers if they sag. Without government as referee, worker safety can be compromised. Pollution may be sickening people. Workers might not be paid a living wage (by 2010, taxpayers were actually providing welfare to full-time workers at Walmart while their CEO was making thousands per hour – not to mention the Waltons). Workers can get fired for organizing unions or whistle-blowing and so it goes.

Corporations can also merge and/or make secret deals to reduce their competition and become more powerful in their markets. They also outsource and offshore jobs to nations with cheaper labor and weaker environmental laws and make use of foreign tax havens. They can thus avoid paying for the infrastructure they use and the military that protects their activities. The bigger the corporations, the bigger government has to be to monitor and enforce laws governing corporations. Shouldn't corporations pay the taxes to support this? The U.S. government is not independent enough. The United Nations is not strong enough. (They are lousy referees.)

Sustainable health and peace requires bottom-up government dedicated to self-reliance, fairness, and equal opportunity. Overpopulation precludes this.

In the U.S., self-reliance and bottom-up government are traditional Republican political ideals. Fairness and equal opportunity are traditional Democratic political ideals. We need them together in democratic-republican government. (They only got to be such strongly opposing forces as deregulation led to certain corporate empires with a political agenda getting into news broadcasting.)

Make no mistake – we need institutional government for a sustainable civilization of maximized health and peace. The primary purpose of government, however, cannot be taking care of people (Democrats?) or taking care of big investors and their corporations (Republicans?). The purpose of government needs to be to promote and protect social and environmental conditions such that all able people can civilly take care of themselves.

Such self-reliance does create diverse people. This makes socialization and education and ongoing information in democracies all the more important if diverse individuals are to be naturally motivated toward values that benefit everyone. This includes not overpopulating their habitats. (When overpopulated, they naturally compete for selfish goals or get homogenized by top-down empire leadership.)

Democracy occurs naturally in small, cohesive communities of people when a special situation or necessary project calls for coordinated efforts. Most everyone already recognizes who is most qualified to lead and "votes" for him or her. Otherwise, adults in such small communities can normally govern themselves according to the "tried and true" values of diversity within group boundaries. In larger societies, too, a people's democracy will work best, that is, provide optimal freedom, justice, health, and peace, if it is bottom-up (not top-down) in power structure.

Bottom-up democracy is decentralized democracy.

Bottom-up government means the bottom layer is composed of all stakeholders sufficiently socialized, educated, and continuously informed to, first of all, govern themselves individually with values of health and peace. Secondly, they can better recognize the best people to elect (for their ideas and expertise – not looks and popularity) in each next upper level of government (the republican piece) to make decisions on their behalf.

Bottom-up also means that each next upper level of government only exists to solve any problems that the level immediately below is unable to solve. The most important problem-solving layer is the first layer of individuals who govern themselves. Next in importance is the second level immediately above them (community governing bodies). These elected representatives only meet to tackle any problems that individuals can't solve themselves (and will be closest to the problem for the likely best solution). The third tier of government only meets to solve any problem that the tier immediately below them could not get solved and so it goes through county, regional, state, and national governments on up to an absolutely necessary world-governing body. (We all share the same planet.) While a world government would be the most far-reaching elected level of government, that power should only be used (says a world constitution and world courts) if all government layers below are unable to solve a particular problem concerning world health or peace (like overpopulation or global warming).

This bottom-up model is truly a republican democracy (think Thomas Jefferson) and minimizes (term-limits can help) the addiction-to-power goings-on most prevalent with top-down government (even when called a democracy).

Governments, bottom-up in power, will only work with right-sized and stable populations per habitat.

That's when uniting values of cooperation for health and peace, not power over others, can and will be the norm. (It's in our DNA.)

The right top-down leadership could certainly make a big difference, especially with today's overpopulation and environmental issues or when a nation's cultural/economic system is at fault (think Gorbachev collapsing the Soviet Union). More often than not, however, big, top-down government inevitably becomes part of the problem (like currently in the U.S. – it's the power-addiction and entitlement thing).

The most important government functions are to maintain the social requirements and ecological environments necessary for self-reliance in local economies to continue indefinitely. These conditions start with relevant education and information for all plus an effective population policy keeping numbers in balance with habitat resources and opportunities for self-development. Then all organizations (especially private investor-owned corporations) can be easily regulated by bottom-up government and working foremost for the common social and ecological good. There would be no incentives to continually expand in size.

When sustainable conditions are established for mostly local self-reliance in local economies, the upper levels of government do not even have to meet on a regular basis. Their office holders (think public servants) can be elected volunteers with only their expenses paid. This is good and sustainable government that doesn't go broke for lack of tax revenue.

Bottom-up democracies still need constitutions spelling out the boundaries for protecting basic individual (self-reliant) rights to keep them from being voted away or otherwise taken by any majority (though not very likely with the non-competitiveness of right-sized and stable populations).

In keeping with bottom-up democracy, it's really up to each of us to support and promote the three necessary cultural commitments for global health and peace.

For a democratic-republic to be effective and sustainable, the most government must take place at the bottom (citizen) level so that each next higher level has less governing to do and the top (world) level has the least. While good leaders (not empire-builders) in good organizations can help tremendously, the key players for a sustainably good life of health and peace are "we, the people." With sufficient socialization, education, and ongoing information, they, collectively, make sustainably healthy, peaceful community life happen. And enough such communities make for a sustainably healthy, peaceful nation while enough such nations make for a sustainably healthy and peaceful world.

It is really up to each of us (including CEOs of big corporations) to govern ourselves in ways that contribute to the sustainable health and peace we want for our kids and grandkids. I'm also saying that requires (1) working to make relevant, science-based health and peace education and ongoing information taught and communicated around the globe, particularly about the need for (2) contraception and family planning (as in *The Legacy Rule*), and (3) the need to be moving toward mostly self-reliance in local economies governed by bottom-up democracies.

Modern cultures are now so complex as well as steeped in instant gratification or short-term gains that these three cultural commitments may sound like laughable idealism. We simply can't afford to collectively live otherwise and have sustainable health and peace. There is no real alternative. These three objectives reinforce each other in a system of gradual change that would diminish every social problem we experience or hear about in our (sensationally negative) commercial news media. And everyone, with awareness and knowledge, can act every day in ways that further them.

As we work towards these requirements for sustainable health and peace, I am also saying to not vote for or support any government office-holders that would have us carry on at home or abroad like an empire.

Only support government of the people, by the people, and for the people. You are part of that. Such government is necessary to maintain the conditions (protect the commons) that make the most freedom (self-reliant living) possible within the bounds of sustainable civilization.

But peacefully oppose and hold accountable empire-building government leaders. . .

1. Who do not support and promote secular, science-based education and independent information for all citizens as the highest priority.
2. Who do not support and promote population policies geared for the carrying capacity of citizen habitats, nor provide the knowledge and means for achieving them.
3. Who are against stronger democratic ("majority rules") voting and republican (bottom-up) government structure. Actually, the U.S. has one of the weakest democracies in the world. We need to get rid of the Electoral College, correct the dysfunctional Senate, and reform election administration, gerrymandering, and campaign financing, among other things.
4. Who are against protecting basic individual human rights from the "tyranny of the majority" and might vote against those rights for certain minority groups and/or not protect those rights from the tyranny of empire-builders who want to control citizens thinking and doing to favor their empire.
5. Who do not represent the people – who collude with rather than regulate special interests and would-be empire-builders in business or religion or whatever (and who do much of the public's business in secret).

Peacefully oppose and hold accountable empire-building government leaders. . .

6. Who tax the wealthy and privileged at lower rates than everybody else with the faulty promise of "trickle-down" economics. Trickle-down economics is a model for family economics – the better off the parents, the better the prospects of their children. Neither governments nor corporations acting as our parents are realistic. It is not good for us or them and history shows only the rich get better off – way better off.
7. Who do not see that their sick or disabled and most vulnerable citizens are cared for.
8. Who get power "fixes" by fabricating or exaggerating danger in order to justify needless military spending and perpetually going to war for power and profits.
9. Who waste taxpayer's money by developing bloated, wasteful, unnecessarily large or obsolete bureaucratic empires operating within administrative agencies of government, duplicating functions or doing for people what they are capable of doing for themselves.
10. Who refuse to support representative world government as needed whenever problems of health and peace within a nation or between nations become too big for them to solve. When we can get it, representative world government can best stand up to any international corporate, religious, or political empires dysfunctional for world health and peace (as is currently the case).

The United Nations is "toothless" largely because leaders in the United States and "competing" nations refuse to give up any power over their sovereignty. (The U.S. can afford to go first – they can always take it back.)

As we work toward the requirements for sustainable health and peace, do not automatically be against all organized religion.

Religions were the first organizations to reunite people in values of civility after overpopulation set in. With daily and weekly rituals (reminders), they help keep people united with the cultural values that promote health and peace. Religious organizations have long cared for the sick and aided the poor in countless ways around the world, most especially in war and after disasters. Religious organizations offer the benefits of community and are in the best position to provide the spiritual sustenance that makes a positive difference for troubled souls (stories and beliefs compatible with health and peace do not have to be proven true to be of value).

Peacefully oppose organized religious empires and hold accountable any leaders. . .

1. Who carry on as though they possess the only true religion or teach that the non-religious are, by definition, bad people.
2. Who say they are appointed by God rather than democratically elected by members.
3. Who trap themselves in a "tyranny of certainty" by maintaining obsolete beliefs, creeds, and dogma that ignore or deny evolving knowledge about Nature (ecology) and human nature (biology and psychology).
4. Who discourage or forbid exposure to outside ideas and information, religions, or philosophies.
5. Who forbid sex education and contraception to promote larger families for membership growth. Larger families mean more stress and more stress can better fill houses of worship. (And who pays for the increasing social burden in overpopulated habitats?)

Peacefully oppose organized religious empires and hold accountable any leaders. . .

6. Who keep women in inferior, second-class roles in religious participation and leadership.
7. Who preach "put your life in God's hands" (as interpreted by clergy) rather than take responsibility for one's own life. This helps stifle individual potential and diversity for easier control of members' thinking and doing.
8. Who use shame, fear, and the threat of punishment, (as in sinful, sinner, the devil, hellfire and damnation) to gain the compliance of young followers. (I think churches do best as places of comfort, not judgment.)
9. Who define God as a father or parent figure who runs the world and looks at the world's people like children who are blessed only when they do His bidding (as interpreted by the leaders). I think defining God as Nature or the Higher Power of the universe is more logical and healthiest.
10. Who take advantage of freedom of religion to try to become the dominant or sole religion (that competition and power thing) and want to do away with diversity and secular democracy.

Yes, there really are religious organizations free of these disqualifiers – my favorites are Unitarian-Universalist Congregations, also Quakers, also some Buddhism, Hinduism, and Baha'i groups. More and more liberal branches and offshoots of many Christian and Islamic organizations can be found with leaders who are seekers of knowledge and not afraid of change to increase universal health and peace.

In working toward universal health and peace in today's world, corporate empires are most in need of being checked and regulated for the public good.

Corporate heads tend to view their money-making decisions as amoral. Unfortunately, that amorality gets to be immorality. They use what they gain, wealth, power, and privilege, to increase their probability of gaining more and more and more. Soon they can then buy out or force out their weaker competition, including local businesses and start-ups. They can, in time, control state and national governments – even in democracies, if they can own enough news media, lobbyists, and politicians.

A people's government might make changes and better regulate their "amorality" rather than have taxpayers picking up the resulting costs to society (crime, welfare, pollution, crumbling infrastructure from empire use). So, corporate empire-builders, at least, in the U.S., want to make citizens think it's their government that is at fault when the economy is not doing well. They want more "free markets" and "free trade."

Since the 1980s, in the U.S., the interests of investor-owned corporations have been well represented in the U.S. Congress, in the Reagan, Clinton, and George W. Bush presidencies, and, worst of all, on the U.S. Supreme Court.

In the U.S. and much of the world, we have too many huge corporations controlling people and their governments for private gain instead of people and their governments controlling corporations for the common good. The biggest investor-owned corporations end up with global power to decide who gets what opportunities and resources for how much, forcing more and more irrelevant nations, states, communities, and their citizens to the margins or out of the game. It is not democracy. It does not foster peace in the world.

Corporate empires are now the most popular venue for wealth and power addiction. They and their investors are the "establishment."

While the U.S. Constitution does not mention rights of corporations, "We the People of the United States of America, etc." has "evolved" to include corporations as people.

From its beginning, corporate-minded presidents and corporate interests in Congress realized that they could become more powerful with sympathetic judges appointed to the courts. And so they did, while not enough citizens paid attention along the way. It seems the majority of justices on the U.S. Supreme Court have been liberal enough to favor people over big corporations only 30-some years out of the last 150. (That was following The Great Depression.)

1789 – The U.S. Constitution was put into effect.

1819 – The U.S. Supreme Court ruled that corporate charters were really contracts. This gave them legal standing under the Constitution. (Dartmouth College vs. Woodward)

1886 – In recording a U.S. Supreme Court ruling that private corporations were entitled to due process under the law (Fourteenth Amendment), a court clerk inserted words that said corporations were, in effect, like human beings. This began a legal precedent that the Court let stand. (Santa Clara County vs. Southern Pacific Railroad)

1906 – The U.S. Supreme Court gave corporations Fourth Amendment protection against search and seizures by the government. (Hale vs. Henkel)

1919 – The U.S. Supreme Court let stand a Michigan court ruling that the primary purpose of private corporations is not to serve the public good, but to maximize profits for its stockholders. (The seeds for The Great Depression, and a whole lot more, were sown.)

1922 – In a most intimidating ruling for "government of the people" to keep corporate activities compatible with health and peace, the U.S. Supreme Court interpreted the "Takings Clause" of the Fifth Amendment to mean that not just property, but profits lost to corporations because of government laws had to be compensated. (Pennsylvania Coal v. Mahon)

1976 – The U.S. Supreme Court ruled that freedom of speech (First Amendment) includes spending money – like in political campaigns – those with the most money get the most speech. (Buckley v. Valeo)

2010 – The corporate majority on the U.S. Supreme Court affirmed the above and ruled that corporations have the same rights as citizens under the First Amendment and government cannot restrict their spending on elections. (Citizens United v. Federal Election Commission)

More First Amendment constructionism has followed, including decisions in 2014 that "family" corporations, in effect, have religious rights that can outweigh government laws.

These decisions upset the balance of power inherent in our Constitution. There is no way that citizens can match the spending clout and the molding-public-thinking expertise of today's corporations in political campaigns (like with news media management, video productions, attack ads, and publicity). And, so far, they can do much of their political power grabs anonymously.

Corporations, by getting their people elected in federal, state, and city levels of government, including their judiciary, can control their relationship "contracts" with employees, with customers, and with local communities. They can control these contracts with profits for their shareholders coming first. (Sustainable health and peace actually interferes with profit-making.) And, for all practical purposes, we now have government of corporations, by corporations, and for corporations.

On the other hand, do not automatically be against the idea of private, investor-owned corporations.

Private corporations, with generating profits as their capital-raising incentive, originally lifted living standards for about everyone. And they do better at manufacturing a host of products that lend themselves to self-reliance in local economies. They do need to be tightly regulated by people's governments if not locally owned. And their profits need to be taxed sufficiently to pay for all social and environmental costs, to contribute to the public good, and to limit their expansion. Ideally, all investors should have to work for a living (just like people with no money to spare) so that interest and dividends received are more like "dessert" – not their main, gluttonous-producing menu.

Peacefully oppose and hold accountable private, investor-owned corporate empires and their leaders. . .

1. Who get big and powerful enough to run "mom & pop" and family retail stores out of business by gaining government favors, getting volume discounts from suppliers, undercutting prices, and monopolizing markets.
2. Who strive to undermine self-reliance in local communities by getting between citizens and their needs so as to take over, control, hoard, ration, and profit from what local citizens could better provide for themselves.
3. Who make the environment ugly and/or pollute air, water, and soil with waste – compromising and destroying the ecosystems necessary for healthy self-reliance.
4. Who erode "we, the people" social democracy with their propaganda, their lobbying, their campaign practices for getting their people elected and appointed, also their secret alliances to influence or by-pass government.

Peacefully oppose and hold accountable private, investor-owned corporate empires and their leaders. . .

5. Who strive to keep voters thinking government is the enemy in order to keep themselves unregulated. Governments can be voted out – big corporations not exactly.)
6. Who are so huge and complex that they cannot be regulated, taxed, fined, or shut down by any government as in "too big to fail."
7. Who refuse to pay a living wage to their employees, even forcing them to get government welfare while employed full time, especially obscene when their CEOs/owners/stock holders are profiting mightily. (Check Walmart's and McDonald's record on this, for example.)
8. Who do not maintain adequate safety and health standards for their workers or the communities in which they operate.
9. Who use "trick and trap" misleading, unfair and unethical fine-print agreements and contracts for installment buying, loaning money, and providing credit accounts.
10. Who exist solely to maximize the profits of their shareholders and have no provisions in their charters or management structure to include all stakeholders affected by their activities, namely employees, suppliers, communities, society-at-large, and future generations.

In 1952, 35% of government revenue came from corporations. By 2012, thanks to the evasive schemes of their lobbyists, accountants, and lawyers, it was less than 10%. But they are still the heaviest users of U.S. public infrastructure as well as our police and military to protect their asse(t)s. The 1980s' Reagan Revolution was really a corporate revolution, well-assisted by Far Right Conservatives on the U.S. Supreme Court. I cannot over-emphasize how much power super-rich business investors and their corporate conglomerates now have for controlling governments and preying on the world's people to feed their addictions.

Conservation is the true calling of conservatives. We need such conservatives like never before.

We need conservatives pushing for self-reliance (including for conditions that make it possible). We need them pushing for bottom-up government (including reducing the power of Wall Street banks and big corporations). We need them pushing for balanced budgets (including raising progressive tax revenue to pay for past wars and Pentagon budgets).

Times change – democracy needs to always be a work in progress. Some ways today's "conservatives" are helping preserve the status quo and thereby harming the future of our children, grandchildren, and great grandchildren.

1. Continually cutting taxes that support public schools and colleges and specifically opposing sex education.
2. Opposing science, specifically the need to combat overpopulation and global warming.
3. Opposing family planning and non-profit Planned Parenthood Clinics which have been providing reproductive health services, mainly to poor women, since 1916.
4. Opposing gun safety laws and encouraging the proliferation of ever more powerful guns.
5. Supporting an ever-growing military and an ever-growing for-profit, military arms and technology industry.
6. Investing in, buying, and promoting ever bigger and faster consumer products – houses, cars, boats, and all the latest possible technology regardless of environmental and social consequences.
7. Opposing recycling and pollution prevention as in "It will hurt the economy."
8. Never listening to public news media or views other than their traditional beliefs and never compromising on them.
9. Conducting politics as though winning is the absolute highest priority and, therefore, any way possible justifies it.
10. Voting for Far Right (not-normal Republican) candidates and policies which, since 1980, have the "best" record of concentrating power in fewer and fewer hands for corporate, religious, and political empire-building.

A "responsibility follows" page.

- If we are going to have a well-functioning democratic-republic, then we have to have a well-functioning, non-partisan, non-commercialized public education and information system for current and future voters. Democracy needs open-minded dialogue to see who has the best ideas to build on, not fabricated attack ads, confrontation, and winning power plays to see who gets their way.
- If we have to have big private investor-owned corporations competing with each other to make money in a healthy, peaceful society, then we should have them taxed to pay for big independent government to regulate their ethics.
- If we are going to have big private investor-owned corporations automating and robotizing and off-shoring away jobs to make more money, then we should have them taxed to pay for the welfare needs of the unemployed and underemployed they leave behind.
- If air, water, or soils aren't clean enough for healthy living because corporate investors made/make more money polluting them, then we should regulate them better and have them pay to restore healthy air, water, and soil.
- If there are big private investor-owned corporations that can only stay in business with an ever increasing population, or by getting rid of jobs, or by polluting the environment, or by using (abusing) our freedoms to take over local, state and federal governments, then we should not have them stay in business.
- If the people's government doesn't have enough power over big private investor-owned corporations to remedy the above situations, then the people have the choice of simplifying their lifestyles (requires smaller families) for less corporate consumption and more local independence so as to regain control over their economic system (and their health, peace, and sustainability).

(Check out Newman's Own or Ben & Jerry's Ice Cream or Certified B Corporations.)

Signs of failing civilization (in my book).

1. When its police departments are becoming more militarized with equipment and training that makes them more like combatants than guardians and peacekeepers.
2. When that special place in Nature where people from past generations went to find the most peace-of-mind has been replaced for present generations by a strip mall or an apartment complex.
3. When commercial radio and television heads refuse to run ads for condoms, contraception, or small families, or population policies, or conservation of resources.
4. When contraception, masturbation, and even coitus interruptus, are still forbidden sins by many religious empire-builders.
5. When a religious leader (Pope Paul VI) overruled a "Papal Commission on Population and Birth Control," made up of physicians, psychologists, sociologists, married couples, and Catholic clergy, who, after three years of study and debate, voted 69 to 10 that the Church's prohibition on contraception be annulled. This was in 1966 when the world's population was still at a sustainable number (3 billion) for its finite resources. (And, at this writing, it's still forbidden.)
6. When U.S. citizens elect presidents (like Far Right Hero Ronald Reagan or George W. Bush) who deregulate corporate empires and fight environmentalism, environmental science, and family planning.
7. When population and environmental concerns have gone from being bipartisan, no-brainer issues (in the United States in the 1970s) to being opposed by most every Republican in politics with Democratic campaigners afraid to bring it up.

8. When it has more slavery now than ever before (people who have no other options but to do a master's or boss's bidding for food and shelter or for the means, dictated by the employer, to purchase them).

9. When many of its children miss out on realistic education for taking care of themselves, their social and physical environment, their democracy, or no longer get enough exercise, have little safe "free-range" playtime, or are homeless, go hungry, starve.

10. When the lack of future health and happiness in life can already be accurately predicted in a child by the age of three (and a privatized prison industry plans accordingly).

11. When its "national pastime" went from civilized baseball to uncivilized football. The game of baseball didn't change. People changed. They now get bored with baseball and enjoy athletes trying to injure each other. (Roman Coliseum stuff all over again.)

12. When the competition between ideas and creations in its culture has regressed into competition between people – for opportunities to develop themselves into idea thinkers and creation makers – or just to have a decent life.

13. When more of its people are opposing other people to get their way instead of opposing their ideas in informed debates and then democratically voting.

14. When explicit violence, which is about pain and the destruction of life, is far more widely accepted, even welcomed in its entertainment, than explicit sex, which has to do with pleasure and the creation of life.

15. When guns and weapons of war are a growth industry for the public and not enough people can tell the difference between gun safety and gun ownership.

16. When fewer of its citizens value science or understand evolution than did so 50 years ago.

17. When too many of its people have made up their minds ahead of time that they know truth and automatically ignore or dismiss further reasoning, information, and evidence to the contrary.

18. When its public education systems have been so marginalized that too many of its citizens are more influenced by rigid political, corporate, or religious ideology and threatened by opposing research data, diversity, and compromise (the very hallmarks of democracy).

19. When an adult generation's favorite reading materials or films are more about dragons, vampires, zombies, and outer-space aliens than real people and real-life events in the real world.

20. When each generation's most popular music is less musical than the last (and louder) – and highly paid singers use auto-tune.

21. When its young people have to either have wealthy parents or gamble on whether going heavily into debt for college tuition will get them a place at the economic table (and then they still can't buy a house).

22. When its young people are flocking to inner city apartments because they cannot afford to own a house like their parents – as young people started doing several thousand years ago when they could no longer get a plot of land of their own for agrarian livelihood like their parents.

23. When most of its people must subordinate and prostrate themselves to the regimentation and benevolence of empire-builders in corporations, governments, or organized religions to have identity, feel secure, or just to survive.

24. When more of its economic participants must sit for eight or more hours a day staring at a little box in spite of overwhelming evidence that it is unhealthy behavior.

25. When more of its people have to turn to (top-selling) prescription drugs for anxiety and depression (or street drugs) because they are unable to change their lifestyles.

26. When huge corporate conglomerates, with profit-making as their defining purpose, are the primary shapers of its economic culture (the highest values being determined by whatever makes the most money most quickly).

27. When its economy and culture are based mostly on ever expanding development and consumption of natural resources instead of sustainable conservation.

28. When its business and government leaders are able to privatize corporate profits and socialize corporate costs and losses, even to future, yet-to-be-born generations.

29. When the growing costs of its education, childcare, and medical care are not matched by growing salaries and wages, thereby shrinking most of its middle classes toward financial insecurity.

30. When its primary ongoing communication and information systems necessary for intelligent citizenship are controlled by a half dozen private corporate media conglomerates using sensationalism and validation of existing market biases to enhance their profit margins.

31. When its government policy-makers listen more to economists and business moguls than to ecologists and social scientists or are amassing government debt for the next generations while trying to make the unrealistic economy work for everyone and/ or helping those left out.

32. When multitasking (requires shallow thinking) has become necessary to hold a job or get through the day instead of mindful unitasking (allows for deep thinking).

33. When its citizens are taught that its economy depends on the few richest and most powerful (past winners of competition or their offspring) getting even richer and more powerful in order to provide trickle-down livelihood for the rest (and too many believe it).

34. When its fewer rich citizens end up owning more and more assets and resources while the many non-rich end up more and more doing their work or doing without.

35. When its economy is actually rigged by a money supply system based on debt and interest so that wealth actually bubbles up from the work and risks of those below to the already super-wealthy at the top.

36. When its wealthy citizens pay a lower percentage of their income in taxes than the non-wealthy and an income gap grows between them.

37. When its leaders and their followers promote and protect social classes of entitlement (deservedness) based on criteria other than individual effort, ability, and talent expressed.

38. When its legislatures give more power and tax breaks to the industries that pollute than to the interests of clean air and water and healthy soil.

39. When its majority Supreme Court judges ignore the balance of powers principle that its government was founded on and declare that corporations and religious organizations are equal to individual people in Constitutional rights.

40. When winning is more important than truth and its political campaigns are made up of deliberate lies and outright fabricated stories presented in clever, mind-manipulating videos produced by unnamed sources. (We now have fact-free elections.)

41. When the losing opposition after an election blocks or sabotages every move by the winning party (and is able to) so the winners are blamed for nothing getting done.

42. When its corporate-backed politicians (in the U.S.) can use computer-generated gerrymandering to choose their voters instead of voters choosing their politicians as well as making voting more difficult for certain classes of voters, thereby bypassing democracy.

43. When its beautiful, resource-abundant areas are allowed to become over-developed, over-crowded, resource-depleted, and ugly and its capitalists then take the money they made and move on to the next beautiful, resource-abundant place to do the same, maybe until the whole world is ugly (except behind the gated and guarded communities where the capitalists live and vacation and locals compete to serve them and do their work).

44. When it spends more money on law enforcement and prisons for its left-out and rebellious young people than on their opportunities, teachers, and schools of higher education (and those prisons are overcrowded).

45. When extremist groups are increasing who never compromise, never give up, and believe their ends justify any means.

46. When "all's fair in love and war" becomes "all's fair in love, war, politics, and economics" and the U.S. Supreme Court helps make it so.

47. When the death penalty is getting used more often (and in spite of the numbers of post-convicted, DNA-established innocent people found on "death row").

48. When it spends more money on research and weapons for its military to maintain its status quo than on research and aid toward the needs for world health and peace.

49. When too many of its estrogen-blessed young women have just two choices for fitting into society: use their sex appeal or have babies. The two can often seem like only one (no) choice.

50. When too many of its testosterone-blessed young men have only two choices for discharging their natural energy: do anti-social-criminal activity or join a religious-political-military crusade against demonized enemies. The two can often seem like only one (no) choice.

51. When it is so crowded, complicated, and stressful to go out and experience real life that more and more people elect to stay in when they can and have virtual life come to them via digital electronics.

52. When most of its biggest businesses ignore ecological capital. Most of its recreation excludes Nature. Most of its living does not take place in the real world and most of its lifestyles do not fit reality.

To make a long story short – a summary:

Human-like primates in Africa evolved into homo sapiens maybe 400,000 years ago. By about 200,000 or more years ago, survival of the fittest had them well adapted to their natural habitats in terms of climate, geography, water and food sources, microbes, parasites, predators, and giving birth. Just two to four hours a day of hunting and gathering made their societies the healthiest, sexiest, and most relaxed Planet Earth ever knew. (This is in the DNA of all of us.) They didn't need agriculture, industry, or technology (well, maybe better contraception). After about 140,000 more years of this "Garden of Eden" living, they began slowly spreading their numbers into the Middle East, Asia, Europe, and beyond to prevent overpopulation.

In time, however, most natural human habitats did get too full of people with no new unclaimed habitats to easily find. Big changes occurred, well underway by about 10,000 years ago. One was the development of agriculture to increase the food-supply. This made possible even more (too-many) people. Agricultural-supported settlements grew into towns and towns into cities.

As cities grow with excess people, they require food and materials and supplies to be hauled in from elsewhere whether elsewhere likes it or not. Thus began a history of cities and nations of them fighting each other as well as encroaching into the lands of subsistence farmers and the remaining peaceful, vulnerable hunting and gathering societies around the globe. This resulted in the development of urban empires to out-compete the lesser or unorganized and conquer, intimidate, and oppress them for needed resources and labor. So, in the last 10,000 years, much of life-loving humanity has instead endured much conflict and violence and war between themselves and between their groups to see who gets control (ownership) over what territory. They also got slavery, pollution, and plagues of diseases mutating from their concentrations – a whole lot of suffering going on. The real problem was/is too many people.

As time went by, many influences (including discovery of an entire underpopulated continent) got this situation improving with science, engineering, printing presses, public education, capitalism, a labor movement, and emerging democracy (rule of people's law over rule of power). Thus began the industrial-technological age and higher material standards of living for potentially everyone. Unfortunately, it was answered with much, much more overpopulation. Much, much more overpopulation made all the more competition and empire-building, especially as the winners could use their added power for expansion to better secure self-serving supplies and feed addictions. And still there were wars, even worldwide wars, over who controls whom and what resources. This, in turn, set up alliances and monetary policies to create monopolies for more power and profit (while the population kept multiplying in urban areas providing ever cheaper labor). Most democracies eroded into mostly established corporate-elite, behind-the-scenes rule. With their lobbyists and power over communications, wealth-addicted capitalists have mostly jettisoned labor unions and begot economic globalization and automation and robotics with growing unemployment and underemployment, homelessness, and hunger among the excess of people. This has divided the world into controlling winners and power-less non-winners (haves and have-nots) with a majority of young people in the latter group (many of which are joining gangs and terrorist groups).

Now the biggest winners manage corporate economies larger than the economies of half the nations on Earth. With profits to shareholders as their highest purpose, they are exploiting scarcity and undercutting local economies around the world. The planet's ecologies are going dysfunctional from air, water, and soil pollution. The planet's governments are going broke dealing with wild weather, wars, welfare, and refugees. Civilization is poised to come apart while we are supposed to just get bigger, tougher, faster, smarter than our competitors. I'm sorry, but we're in deep shit, People! There are too many of us.

The last best time for a population policy was 30 years ago; the next best time is now.

For hunting and gathering to be sustainable, wild food sources had to expand along with the population. They didn't. For subsistence farming to be sustainable, the amount of fertile land had to expand along with the population. It doesn't. For the industrial and technological age to be sustainable, the abundance of raw materials and non-renewable resources had to expand along with the population. They aren't.

In the United States, the following government population policy would do the job:

1. Provide the funds for and make mandatory in all secondary schools a complete sex education curriculum that emphasizes the need for family planning and contraception. (At this writing less than half the states have any sex ed.)
2. Carry on a public information campaign about the necessity of reducing population, including a target population number for sustainability and periodic reporting of progress.
3. Provide free contraceptives, "morning-after" pills, vasectomies, and tubal ligations to all who desire them.
4. Give the same tax breaks (social relief) to couples with zero children or one child as are given for two children. Stop all tax subsidies for more than two children beginning with new births nine months from the date of legislative passage.
5. Close off the borders to illegal immigration and have all future immigration maintained by lottery to match emigration out of the country. Note that temporary asylum for refugees is a separate (humanitarian) issue.

With overpopulation, only the rich and their lackeys keep winning (until all hell breaks loose). With right-sized populations everybody wins enough. The more industrious and talented can still win more (without getting addicted to wealth and power) and generations that follow have the same prospects for winning.

The following organizations concerned with overpopulation are good sources of information and can use our financial support. (There are more as well.)

- Blue Planet United
- Negative Population Growth
- Planned Parenthood Federation of America
- International Planned Parenthood Federation
- Population Connection
- The Population Council
- Population Matters
- Population Media Center
- Population Reference Bureau
- Population Services International
- World Overpopulation Awareness

July 11th of every year is World Population Day. Is your community doing something to draw attention to the overpopulation issue? How about organizing "teach-ins," like young people did about the Vietnam War?

Invite everyone to regularly check the United Nations' World Population Clock online. We are currently adding five more new babies every two seconds. (It's about one new baby every second in the U.S.) They all deserve a future of living, loving, working, and recreating in health and peace. But when there are too many, how is the choice made for who gets to learn how and who doesn't? And who gets the necessary resources and who doesn't? To let it be winners of competition is a cop-out. If that's the best we can do, I wouldn't call ourselves civilized. We need to reverse that clock, in part by repeatedly spreading, promoting, following *The Legacy Rule*.

This could be considered the third ending to this book.

However, I'd like to cover what makes for psychologically maturing people (who don't need to be under the rule of political, corporate, or religious empires).

The full impact of overpopulation.

When there are too many of any species for the natural carrying capacity of their given habitat or ecological niche, they are prevented from maturing to their fullest potential. Plant too many carrots in a row without thinning and none grow to their potential. (The two on the ends do better.) When there are too many deer in a forest (not enough predators), they all become stunted and unhealthy (after severely degrading their habitat and before opportunistic diseases start killing them off).

If a farmer keeps some pigs in a large pasture with plenty of natural food, they will not make him as much money compared to penning them up and feeding them. Confined, each will become greedy and gluttonous, compete to eat more than the others and gain more weight by market time. They will also bite off each other's tails from the stress of getting in each other's way. (They become a pain in the ass to each other.) Too many rats in an enclosed experimental environment, even when the food supply is kept plentiful, develop unbelievable antisocial and bizarre behaviors competing with each other for space to be their undisturbed selves.

Humans confined in overcrowded habitats are no exception. A basic law of psychology is that behavior is strengthened or weakened by its consequences. Habitats of humans continually getting in each other's way (the consequences of too many people) produce cultures and economies (lifestyle habits) different from how we are designed by Nature to live. That gives way to crime, mental illness, suicides, and addictions. (And who is profiting from the greed and gluttony that develops in all that competition for paychecks, for space, for identity?)

The following model explains how overpopulation affects psychological maturing.

The hierarchy of needs for psychologically healthy humanity.

Evolution gives us genes for a range of subhuman to immature to mature human behaviors. Which genes blossom depends on the environmental/social conditions stimulating their expression. Psychologist Abraham Maslow first postulated a hierarchy of needs to be met before anyone could approach self-actualization – his term for psychological maturity. (In science, a theory attempts to make sense out of a whole lot of data – research continues to support Maslow's theory.)

The first level of need is basic to physical survival. Daily fresh air, safe drinking water, nutritious food, sufficient sleep, and adequate warmth (clothing and shelter) have to come first. The second level is the psychological need to feel safe in one's physical and social environment as one goes about securing the needs of the first level.

Too many people per habitat mean some cannot get these needs adequately met, either because there are not enough to go around and they keep losing in the competition or violence or the winner-take-all greed that develops.

At the third level of importance are the social-psychological needs that come from relationships: childhood acceptance and bonding (to non-stressed-out parents), and, then, as adults, a sense of belonging in a community, being sexual, and enjoying loving adult to adult relationships.

It's a double-whammy. Chronically cold, starving, and sick children and adults who are also feeling insecure and fearful (not getting the first and second need levels on the list) are typically unable to form the kinds of relationships (the third level) that keep them growing psychologically. Their relationships remain more attachment avoidant or continue more like a child with a supposed parent (care-giver or protector) even in adulthood. One can see how over-population affects these first three levels in the hierarchy of needs and how it limits advancement beyond them.

The next level of psychological need.

Only if and when these basic physical and relationship needs are adequately and reliably met, are we positioned for gaining the next higher need level – adequate self-esteem. Self-esteem is psychological energy, also referred to as self-confidence or ego strength. Self-esteem basically comes from experiencing more good feelings than bad feelings on average in our daily lives. At this level, it gives us a sense of self-worth that allows us to accept ourselves (warts and all). We have healthy self-respect. Adequate self-esteem is necessary for self-control (will-power) as in "I can do this!" and "I am worth it." Self-control persevering over time toward a worthy goal is often called "grit." Although self-esteem starts building early on from caring relationships and satisfying accomplishments, at higher levels it enables mastery of our skills and possible recognition from peers.

Do not mistake self-esteem for (immature) narcissism (as in "big-ego"). "Know-it-alls" are compensating for a lack of self-esteem. When enough self-esteem is reliably present, self or ego can be dismissed from consciousness.

Self-esteem is the psychological energy individuals need for taking risks with their comfort (or confidence) zone. They can curiously try something new and different and get into a "stretch" zone, then learn and practice at that "place" until their "self" moves into the new, larger comfort zone. This is how we grow and mature psychologically. This is how we become proactive with our choices (self-reliant) for developing our unique selves instead of just following the crowd, or just emotionally reacting to whatever is going on each day, or automatically doing what we are told by "higher-ups" in some empire. Though it should never be severed from Nature or community, this individualism is necessary for progress in civilization.

Self-esteem can certainly be used for ill as well as good, depending on prior learning opportunities (insufficient knowledge and faulty beliefs = the root of all evil), but there likely won't be much payoff energy for higher maturing.

Self-actualization is psychological self-reliance.

We can only get our needs met in the previously described order (each level is a foundation for the next) and when we do so reliably and sufficiently, it actualizes our inherent individuality to the highest level of human functioning. We truly become the best that we can be. Maslow called this entire maturing process "self-actualization." Advancing up the hierarchy of needs actualizes our self's potential. I prefer to call it becoming self-reliant, self-driven by and with enough self-respect (self-esteem) to be responsible for the care and development and wise use of our own unique potential. We are psychologically self-reliant.

At this highest level of human functioning, we use our emotional intelligence, our developed talents, and our accomplished creativity to maintain fulfillment in our lives. Because this highest level embraces empathy and compassion toward others (it's in our DNA), fulfillment for us will naturally include helping to empower others (different than only giving them money or food) and to contribute to society's sustainable civilization. We do this because it feels good and right with our self and adds even more to self's energy (wise use). And we can do this consistently (as in highest level of functioning) because we are coming from a position of strength and maturity. (This is far different than continually trying to outcompete for the thrill of winning more power or financial gain.) "Too many people" per natural habitat gets us off track – only in right-sized populations are most of us able to actualize (mature) our individual selves into reliably empathic and compassionate and unselfish and wise human beings. (It's in our DNA.)

We are self-actualized and practicing self-reliance when we are self-empowered or self-motivated to take charge of our lives. We feel accountable for our own maintenance and our share of social and environmental maintenance. (They can't be separated.) I see being able to be psychologically self-reliant as the top level of self-actualized or mature human development (and evolvement).

Total (physical and psychological) self-reliance.

My definition of total self-reliance has four components. (1) It is a mental set (attitude) that says, "I am in charge of my life." (2) It is sufficient independence and motivation (self-actualization from self-esteem) developed within one's self to meet that responsibility. (3) It is a lifestyle of learned habits and routines (a support system) that one creates and maintains to produce or secure essential needs for self and whatever family one has created, and (4) it is recognizing our interdependence and taking a share of responsibility for maintaining the "greater good" and the "commons." This is the community's, nation's and planet's social and physical environment which we all need for living in healthy and peaceful self-reliance. That includes looking out for others, not out-competing them.

Without enough self-esteem (and resulting self-respect) for mostly practicing self-reliance (or without social-environmental opportunities to acquire enough), we stay mostly dependent on others (like parent-figures or empire-leaders). This does not maximize our psychological health.

We need sufficient self-esteem (self-confidence/self-respect) to take the risks that have us learn (actualize our self) to be self-reliant. Our first doses of good feelings for self-esteem are largely due to others (parents, grandparents, friends, and community). With enough from those sources, we gradually grow psychologically able (have the will-power) to manage our own sources of self-esteem (good feelings) for our own support. That is (total) self-reliance. We have the psychological strength for sufficient self-control to make choices that mostly keep our perceptions, emotions, thoughts, and behaviors good for us, good for our relationships, and good for our social/physical environment. (What's "good" requires sufficient knowledge of human nature and Nature and their relationships as in the first root of healthy, peaceful civilization.)

The main point of this hierarchy of needs concept.

We cannot advance much into the next higher level of functioning until our needs are adequately and reliably met at each of the preceding levels. If we aren't able to get basic survival needs sufficiently met, we will spend most of self's energy on that struggle and not have enough self-esteem to psychologically grow beyond it. And we won't feel very secure. If we do not feel sufficiently safe and secure, we will not have enough self's energy (self-esteem) to authentically fit into our surrounding social group and form healthy adult to adult relationships. (They will be mostly co-dependent.) If we get few relationship needs met, we will never have quite enough self-esteem (self's energy) for the self-discipline (will-power) we need to take risks (have and practice new experiences) that develop our unique, individual potential.

Looking down the hierarchy, people will not get the learning experiences that actualize their unique potential, if they must primarily, mostly rely on others instead of taking the risks themselves (self-reliant). They will not be self-invested as much for psychological growth as for other outcomes. And they will not have the self-discipline or will-power for taking the risks (managing their life and investing in new experiences for self), if they are not getting enough self-esteem from validating and loving adult relationships in their community. And people will not be able to form significant adult to adult relationships, if they are not feeling sufficiently safe and secure. And they will not be able to feel safe and secure if they are continuously sick, hungry, or cold and just trying to survive day to day.

This explains what happens to most people living in poverty. This is what's usually behind the appearance of stupidity or laziness among the poor (which most non-poor use to justify ignoring them when too busy competing to feel compassionate).

Self-reliance is not "going it alone."

I hasten to emphasize that self-reliance (physical or psychological) is not an exclusive or self-sufficiency concept. Individual humans still need communities. And what keeps happening in one community, positive or negative, affects other communities sooner or later. And what keeps happening in a nation of communities, positive or negative, affects other nations, maybe even the entire world, sooner or later. We evolved to be social beings – all in this together.

Healthy individuals will have their roots in Nature, but also in Nature-based communities. People are genetically designed to interact, to mutually support each other, to learn from each other, and to enjoy each other, physically, emotionally, intellectually. We do best having other humans as part of our support system. This is what makes relationship needs the third level of the human need system. Unless a person is extraordinary at relating to Nature, he or she can't develop much psychologically without adult to adult relationships.

While practicing self-reliance, we need to rely on other people secondarily, for safety and security, for reality checks and validation, for knowledge, expertise, and advice, for stimulation, for emotional attachment (love), for sex, for comfort, for cooperation (especially in raising children), for creations and products that maintain healthy living standards, and for times in our life when we become hurt or sick or frail in old age. However, with self-reliance, we retain the right (and the responsibility) to say who, when, how much and for how long we rely on others (and vice versa if others are relying on us).

We evolved to be healthiest when we are sharing ourselves and necessities, but only at the local level can we best determine whether or not we are fostering immature dependence (co-dependence) in our helping and sharing.

Parents are to be in control of children.

What we don't need (if we are to keep maturing psychologically) are people continually in parent-like (authoritarian or autocratic) positions over us after childhood physically ends. Fully developing our individuality is only possible from the stimulation of belonging to a community and is maintained the same way. But healthy communities and societies of them will provide members the freedom to think and do as individuals, so long as they are not a threat to others' freedom to do the same (this should include next generations).

Societies need to foster individual liberty for diversity and to support diversity for all the more quality-of-life ideas and creations which result. Everyone can then learn from them, enhance and build on them, and enjoy their benefits. Individuals need to value society for reality checks on their ideas and creations and to support it in maintaining the social conditions that sustainably encourage individual liberty and diversity. (The "Bill of Rights" in the U.S. Constitution also needs a "Bill of Responsibilities.")

It is only those who prove they are incapable of governing themselves without interfering with other' rights to do the same that need perpetual parents in adulthood. With right-sized population allowing the necessary socialization, education, and ongoing information, their numbers would be practically nil. Unfortunately, their numbers grow with growing overpopulation.

This also says something about the consequences of defining God as a parent taking care of us and managing the world if we obey "Him." (Such a definition has its purpose. Along with monogamy, it is one of the first developments used to maintain order in societies of too many people for self-reliance.) The opposite of happiness is not simply unhappiness, depression, or sadness. It is the lack of control over one's life. (And the concept of heaven after death gives us an out from all that earthly unhappiness.)

Society, with its governments, its corporations, its religions, and other institutions, can mostly help us or mostly hinder, even limit us in actualizing ourselves to self-reliance.

It is the responsibility of society (that's all of us collectively) to maintain the conditions and provide the opportunities necessary for all able people to learn to manage their own lives. That includes deciding when it's in our best interests and society's best interests (they shouldn't be separated) to demonstrate against or deliberately (peacefully) disobey government rulings, or to demonstrate against or withhold the support of certain corporations with our labor, purchases, or investments, and also to do the same with certain religions or their practices. Whether to engage in these acts, depends on whether such institution's educational, social, economic, environmental, and population policies support actualizing self-reliance.

Particularly dangerous to civilization, is society allowing a gap to grow between a few haves and many have-nots when it resorts to competition between people to deal with overpopulation. The lack of opportunities for the have-nots to climb the hierarchy of needs and actualize mature individual self-reliance leaves them vulnerable to recruitment by power-mongering extremist groups with unbending rules for control. At the same time, such groups provide "quick-fixes" to power such as guns, bomb-making instruction, and the idea of possessing a superior religious and/or political philosophy. That killing outsiders and getting killed in the process just gets them to eternal life faster and with higher standing can really be powerful.

Extremist groups raise hell with civilization. Populations right-sized to habitats leave no reason for extremist groups to form.

The relationship of actualized self-reliance to liberty.

The freedom of unstructured play within safe boundaries established by parents and teachers and communities is necessary for a child to keep developing his or her unique potential. It doesn't stop with childhood. As we gain in knowledge and experience so as to remain in the bounds of safety and non-interference with other's rights, we can have the most liberty in adulthood. Freedom and opportunities for pursuing one's own work, hobbies, and interests, not dictated or managed by higher-ups, are necessary to keep one's potential blossoming as adults – within boundaries we can set for ourselves from our own prior education and experience. Sharing habitats peacefully does require putting limits on our liberty (more inhabitants = more limits).

We learn and grow most from having this freedom to make our own decisions as in self-reliance. This certainly includes choosing to negotiate and compromise with others as need be and seeking advice from experts, then deciding whether to follow it or not. We learn and grow less when we have to follow someone else's orders (like leaders of empires) with no freedom of choice. The experience may still be worth-while, but the impact on self is different.

Note: boundaries are best backed up by a wise constitution, and a democratically-elected, bottom-up (republican) government. This is to safeguard our freedom by preventing people from using it to further an agenda that decreases freedom for others, including next generations, as happens (with empire building) in overpopulated habitats.

It follows that we will have much more freedom for self-reliance with right-sized populations. Also, the more complex our lifestyles due to living with overpopulation, the less freedom and self-reliance we will have. Simpler lifestyles are more compatible with Nature and human nature and actualizing potential for self-reliance. Maybe the few hunter/gatherer peoples left among us and their/our similar-living ancestors are/were the wisest people the Earth ever knew.

Freedom to fail, freedom to learn from failure, and freedom to start again are all part of the learning and growing process.

Positive feelings give us psychological energy (self-esteem). Negative feelings drain us of same. Experiencing the positive and negative consequences (feelings) of our own decisions (not some higher-up's) best provides us with the learning needed to secure a continual supply of self-esteem (psychological energy) for more risks and growth. We develop a support system for ourselves.

When you make your own decisions and meet your own challenges, what you learn from your failures and successes and mixed consequences is what most develops your practical and emotional intelligence, your self-awareness (like strengths and weaknesses), your self-control (will-power), your individual character. (This can require more buy-in or more self-investment than just pressing a button or flipping a switch to make things happen.) We get to know, trust, and value our own abilities and resourcefulness as we develop and use them. This self-actualizing makes possible mature adults who don't need parent-like leadership from on high (as in empires). They are self-reliant.

I repeat! Psychological self-reliance definitely includes deciding to consult (or hear or read the words of) experienced friends, parents, grandparents, teachers, mentors, experts, scholars, scientists, and leaders recognized for their insights and wisdom before making certain decisions which are ours to make. (While mistakes have their teaching value, in today's overdeveloped and complex world, the consequences can be horrendous otherwise.)

In any case, we self-actualize (mature) most when we can practice psychological self-reliance, that is, consciously make our own choices for running our lives and recognize, take responsibility for, and learn from the consequences.

I say, more actualizing of self-reliance is what the world's democracies and ecosystems need in its citizens for sustainable health, freedom, fulfillment, and peace.

We still require a support system to maintain ourselves at the self-reliant level of psychological functioning.

I find it most useful to look at one's support system as follows. Basically, there are three areas of variables to "manage" as sources of good feelings (for adequate psychological energy aka self-esteem for the self-control aka will-power needed for self-actualization aka self-reliance). These three areas are your learned habits and routines, your physical body, and your relationships. They all interact in a system that either, on average, mostly supports you (with good feelings) or mostly drains (stresses) you of psychological energy (self-esteem) every single day.

The learned habits and routines area includes thinking habits (like attitudes, beliefs, values, sense of humor, etc.), also emotional connections, work habits and routines, hobbies, interests, recreation-leisure preferences, communication habits, sexual habits, health habits (eating, exercise, relaxation, sleeping, etc.), spending-saving habits, giving and helping habits, and more.

The physical body area includes genetic endowment, nutrition level, fitness level, stress load, discomfort or pain status, brain-body chemistry (includes drugs), immune system, all other aspects of bodily health, and the resulting sum outcome of physical energy.

But we can't do it alone. The relationship area includes a spouse or significant-other, lovers, friends, children, relatives, neighbors, acquaintances, pets, also community home and relationship with Nature or a sense of Higher Power (the same in my book).

Any problem (chronic stressor) in any one of these three areas stands to negatively affect all areas sooner or later if not solved or neutralized. Likewise, any improvement (at providing good feelings) in any one area will improve the other areas sooner or later if lasting.

Making changes with the energy we have.

As a rule, if the "you" inside your body is conscious, you will have energy enough to choose some thought or action that feels good, however brief. And any good feeling strengthens you with more psychological energy. Unless later consequences are more costly in energy, little by little, you can get strong enough to make changes for the better in your support system (better habits, better relationships, better physical health – "better" means they pay off with more net good feelings). As usual, more relevant knowledge and expertise helps. (Educators, counselors, physicians, and therapists can be consulted.)

Self-reliance puts a premium on learning-based sources of good feelings, that is, those created from the learned habits and routines area of your support system. Of the three, that is the area most directly under our control. That kind of learning, though it costs more psychological energy to begin with (acquiring knowledge, skills, and practice first), is like an investment. It pays off more dependably and with more energy (self-esteem) in the long run because you control it.

It follows then that the most reliable sources of self-esteem for supporting self-reliance come from our ability to learn. The learning that starts with opportunities, education, and information from society can proceed with one's self making opportunities, continuing life-long education, and seeking information to better ourselves and society. Through learning and practice, we can replace overstressing habits/routines and strengthen or learn anew, habits which will cost less and pay off more in psychological energy (self-esteem, ego strength) for more self-discipline and self-respect.

The more psychological growth, the more effective (and appropriate) control we have over our support system (our sources of good feelings) and thus our physical and psychological health and strength, for more mature living.

Quick-fix good feelings for psychological energy.

As opposed to learning-based sources of good feelings, quick-fix sources come from outside your self and not so directly within your power to make happen. The best examples of quick-fix sources of good feelings are alcoholic beverages, "recreational" and prescription drugs, being physically attractive, eating sweets, attention after winning competition (different from the training first), spending money (different from earning it), receiving gifts, being taken care of, pampered by others, etc. None of these sources of good feelings actually take much learning or effort from just you as they happen.

By themselves, quick-fixes won't get us enough of the psychological energy (self-esteem) needed for the risk-taking that keeps us learning more self-reliance (growing maturity). Parents – praise your kids for effort and any improvement on past effort, not for winning competition (which also depends on their competitors). Likewise, youth, beauty, gifts, and inheritance, may open some doors (especially in overpopulated areas), but they do not further self-actualization by themselves. They are not accomplishments.

Quick-fix good feeling sources are not automatically bad, however. We had to depend on them as babies and children when we didn't have enough self (or psychological energy) yet developed to take care of ourselves. If we are feeling depressed (not enough psychological energy to do much), they can jump-start us. Nature and human nature have quick-fix sources of good feelings for us in abundance (the simple pleasures of life) if we don't close ourselves off to them with a fast-paced, complex lifestyle (or too much "screen time"). And natural quick-fixes are likely to be free of charge.

Quick-fixes definitely add to our fund of self-esteem, especially if compatible with health and peace. They just require little investment of self and, as such, can be more temporary. They also make us compulsive or tend to be addictive if we primarily rely on them for good feelings.

Examples of differences in sources of good feelings for self-esteem.

On the left are mostly quick-fix types, not necessarily bad. More learning-based sources are on the right. You can recognize which of them will require more initial investment of self (to learn) and result in more reliable sources of good feelings later (as well as more character and maturity).

- Be taken care of --- versus --- practice self-reliance
- Get born with attractive looks --- versus --- develop an attractive personality
- Believe God is running your life --- versus --- believe God (Nature) has given you enough and it's up to you to run your life
- Enjoy a one-night stand --- versus --- cultivate an intimate relationship
- Turn on some digital music --- versus --- play a musical instrument
- Microwave a frozen dinner --- versus --- cook your dinner from scratch
- Have a beer or smoke pot to relax --- versus --- meditate to relax
- Get angry at someone who has offended you --- versus --- try to understand him or her and relate accordingly
- Take a pill for anxiety or depression --- versus --- change your lifestyle habits and support system
- Gamble, speculate, capitalize for income --- versus --- physically labor and create for income
- Buy what you need/want --- versus --- grow/make/build what you need/want

The most culturally universal model for a simple understanding of psychological development.

A valid and reliable support system compatible with the hierarchy of human needs will have individuals naturally absorbing a stream of learning that passes through three distinct stages (learning sets) before actualizing mature self-reliance. They are dependency (childhood), then independency (teen-age and young adulthood), and then being responsible for others (usually learned from parenthood, but also in roles of care providers, teachers, public office holders, managers, therapists, police, etc.). Though they overlap, each learning set contains learned perceptions, thought patterns, emotional connections, and habitual actions mostly consistent with each label and different from the other two. If we keep learning (don't get stuck or fixated in any one stage), we will naturally grow through them and arrive at mature adulthood (self-reliance).

With mature adulthood comes the freedom to forget your own ego or self-esteem needs most of the time (mostly automatic from your support system by then). We also have the most wisdom to pick and choose responses from any of the three learning sets appropriate to any situation. It may be telling your troubles to a close friend or allowing a therapist to help you see what is making you depressed (prompted from your dependent stage). It may be excusing yourself for some time alone to center your self or a vacation to recover your self (coming from your independent learning set). It may be parenting someone by nurturing them or advising them (from your parent self).

However, you are not meant to be forever managed or taken care of (smothered child self), or be carefree with no responsibilities ("spoiled" independent self), or be responsible for others (in a controlling parent role). You can choose to return to full (mature) adult functioning whenever it's best to do so. This puts you in position for a most meaningful, fulfilling life.

The most meaningful, fulfilling, self-reliant life.

You, with psychological energy (self-esteem), are what gives physical energy some direction or purpose. Whenever you don't have to use all your energy for survival or recovery-of-self needs, you can use it to benefit society. Just one instance of being kind and considerate can spread positive energy into the world. A warm smile and greeting can start a positive change in another's entire day and then possibly improve the days of all the whomevers he or she relates to after that. You can actually collect a good feeling for being the kind of person you want to be whether you get a positive response or not from the person you greeted. (It is possible to become too attached to particular outcomes of good works.)

Relating to other people with trust, respect, and regard for their well-being (love) is the best way to get it back and then we have more people with trusting, respecting, loving energy than we had before. And think of what more you can do, more continuously, and for a longer time when the self-reliant "you" doesn't have to worry about survival needs, or social acceptance, or self-esteem issues (because they are so well provided in your support system).

Mature psychological functioning puts you in a position (reserve energy to spare) to help empower others to actualize more self-reliance either by interacting with and helping them directly or doing so indirectly by changing conditions that help open doors for them. Helping to empower others from a position of strength makes us feel even better for more psychological energy to spend on social progress (whether a positive outcome is immediate or taken on faith).

Making the world better is the mainstay of mature, enlightened, self-reliant actualized selves. It provides the most rewarding meaning and purpose to life.

What the hierarchy of needs says about sustainable civilization.

Most important to be aware of, a lack of relevant education and too many people get in the way at every level of this human hierarchical need system. So each of the need levels necessary to get to mature self-reliance is affected by preceding generations (how blessed if they are also mostly actualized, mature, self-reliant people). Previous generations maintaining or restoring social and environmental conditions such that future generations can get through the three stages (learning sets) of development to attain this highest level of functioning would be their greatest gift.

Insufficient knowledge and ever-increasing overpopulation simply prevent more and more people from advancing further and further up the hierarchy of needs to develop their potential. And it sets us up for the kind of competition that leads to undemocratic political, business, or religious empire-builders gaining power and taking over. What a tremendous loss to society that can be and how dangerous that can get.

How many potential Bachs and Beethovens, Franklins and Jeffersons, Dickens and Melvilles, de Vincis and Rembrandts, Edisons and Einsteins, Clara Bartons, Marie Curies, and Margaret Sangers, Martin Luther Kings and Mahatma Gandhis, Ibn al-Rumis and Khalil Gibrans, Guatama Buddhas and Kong Fuzis (Confucius) have come and gone without having been able to develop themselves?

How many became little versions of Hitler or Stalin or Pol Pot or Osama bin Laden instead?

Regression in the hierarchy of needs.

People who are low in self-esteem (never got much to begin with or have too much stress in their lives using it up) are plagued with anxiety and then depression. They don't have the psychological energy to manage their lives and risk doing (stretching) what has them growing psychologically.

Another point to consider is that if people lose their ability to be in charge of their lives because of physical or social changes (like from growing numbers of people), then regression down the hierarchy is also possible. There can be many reasons, especially in competitive conditions of too many people, to have to backtrack and focus on prerequisite needs, even to the extent of temporarily or permanently losing some degree of the self-reliance one has actualized. (If at all possible, we can get it back a whole lot faster.)

While overpopulation at the lower levels can mean too little self-esteem for advancing to the higher levels, overpopulation and its busy, complex lifestyles can also cause too much stress for remaining at the higher levels of functioning. Overstress uses up the self-esteem required. More psychological energy is going out for dealing with or coping with obstacles and problems than coming in.

Too many people and their societies naturally become more competitive, more frustrated, and more violent when stuck at the survival and security beginning of this need hierarchy. This makes supporting an empire-builder attractive in exchange for survival and security needs and some sense of community. A religious empire can help keep the peace. A political empire can better vanquish challengers. A corporate empire can liquidate resources faster for cheaper quick-fixes. But, by definition, empire-builders aren't in it to work themselves out of a job. They aren't going to be using their resources to empower people into sustainable self-reliance. They need to keep feeding their addictions.

The main agenda of established empire-builders.

Because mature, self-reliant individuals don't need empires, empire-builders, subconsciously and consciously, try to keep as many people as possible at the bottom levels of the hierarchy of needs.

Empire-builders seek to get between the people and the opportunities and resources people need for self-reliance and mature adulthood. (This includes opportunities for more liberal education and sexual knowledge.) Empire-builders want to hoard, monopolize, and control the opportunities and resources we need, creating more loyalty and bringing themselves more wealth because of increased demand. Empire-builders can portion resources and opportunities in ways that keep them in power and foster dependency and empire-reliance among people. They traffic in the scarcity caused by overpopulation. They become the gatekeepers people have to satisfy to get somewhere in life – maybe even to survive.

As gatekeepers, empire-builders will reward the most competitive, most assertive or aggressive, most outgoing and attractive people with more opportunities and resources to make them useful and loyal supporters. Subconsciously and consciously, leaders of empires will develop strategies to keep self-esteem and security dependent on them and not coming from sources outside the organization, lest their followers ever begin to think they can make it on their own (self-reliance).

Empire-leaders, as gatekeepers, can extract all manner of support and obedience, loyalty, labor, money, votes, worship, even life from the crowds competing to get whatever benefits their empire has control of. This is the situation when we must live in habitats of too many people.

In the U.S., because a people's government (democratic republic) might stand in the way of corporate empire-builders' agendas, they will use their power to perpetually get taxes cut to weaken government (insufficient budgets = lousy service) and control news and information to make government appear to be the enemy of the people.

If big investor-owned corporate conglomerates (empires) are to have their way in a free society, that society will not remain free.

Corporate empire-builders have created a consumer economy using advertising and growing control of communications and information to groom masses of people to want unnecessary and even unhealthy products just like essentials. (And people tend to not realize they are being so manipulated.)

The marketing schemes of many corporate manufacturing empires are typically to maximize profits by building products with the cheapest construction lasting the briefest time that customers will tolerate (with a new model ready to make the previous one obsolete). This waste, of course, is the exact opposite of what is needed for sustainability. Generally speaking, the bigger the corporation, the worse it is for workers, consumers, the environment, and start-up businesses.

Corporate empires have been allowed to privatize more and more government functions for profit, claiming more "efficiency." It's usually only cheaper at first, the savings borne by workers and the environment. After the captive public is sufficiently accustomed and dependent on the change, the amount they pay climbs with profits into investors' pockets.

Many investor-owned corporations are most interested in privatizing and controlling, for profit-taking, essentials in the hierarchy of needs. That is water, food production, housing, land, socializing (with digital media), as well as education, information, and the Internet. It also includes public safety, medical needs, and pharmaceuticals. (In severely polluted cities, the list can include breathing clean air.)

When empires control people's basic survival needs and opportunities for advancement, people's hearts and minds have a way of following. Then empire-builders control their very identity and potential development (or lack thereof).

Never forget! Promoters of any competition will most likely be the biggest winners of that competition.

A relationship "power game" that handsome and rich men like to play is having two or more women fighting over them. Some attractive women are good at it with men. They can gain lots of extra attention, adoration, pampering, etc., as well as feelings of superiority and entitlement (even without giving up a whole lot of what they seem to promise).

Empire-building arose from overpopulated conditions and over-population helps empire-builders gain more and retain power the same way. Urbanization makes people dependent on providers of essential needs. The heads of empires can get urban people competing with each other for whatever resources and opportunities they control. When an empire's game is the only game in town, followers needing survival, security, acceptance, and/or belonging needs met will compete to be included, also promoted within an empire's hierarchies of power. The empire grows and the leaders benefit from the extra effort as followers try to get ahead of each other to please them. Based on their usefulness, heads of empires will decide who's more worthy and who's not, who can receive benefits and who can't, who's saved and who's damned.

I repeat! It doesn't matter how hard everyone tries, only one person or team can win a contested opportunity and collect what benefits the promoters are giving out. The promoter's strategy is to keep the excluded or "losers" thinking they deserve their loss, but to keep trying and they will win the good benefits sooner or later (or get their good life in heaven after death).

Maybe it's best if participation is voluntary and there are other options for living.

Generally speaking, a more physically self-reliant lifestyle puts a person in the best position for developing psychological self-reliance because of the freedom to set his or her own schedule and agenda.

In our evolving history, physical self-reliance meant building and maintaining a hut among "your people" and going out hunting or gathering food whenever hungry. (Working, buying, consuming day after day is not the same thing – most people have lost their relationship to the land.) In this day and age the closest we can come to physical self-reliance is to own our home (paid for) with enough land and water to be able to organically grow and produce our own food in a community of similarly-living people (who still look out for each other).

The next best situation is owning your home and having your own small business (filling a need for others) reliably providing enough income to buy food from local organic growers and producers. Third best is owning your home while being employed by a needed business for income to buy locally grown organic foods. (These three options, of course, can be in some combination.)

Until the population is reduced sufficiently for small parcels of good land to become available and affordable for most anyone to call home, the following is advisable. As many citizens as can, need to be growing food on lawns, rooftops, balconies, vacant lots, parks, and any available dirt. Become a "gardening angel." Community gardens in cities are a must. Every school should have a garden with students working in it and eating from it. Food co-ops and organic food stores make a valuable difference. Shop at farmer's markets and sign up for subscription produce to help keep local growers in business.

Also, help stop/prevent the loss of good farmland to development any way you can. We will need all of it.

I think the third root of sustainable civilization needs to be that most able individuals practice mostly physical self-reliance in local, cooperative economies to get and stay independent of corporate empire-builders.

This best secures the highest levels in the hierarchy of needs for mature development and functioning (psychological self-reliance) of the citizens of each community.

Since the 1960s, politicians in the United States have implemented many policies and passed much legislation that allowed and encouraged, even coerced people away from mostly physically self-reliant lifestyles toward mostly corporate-reliance for livelihood. Wall Street bankers and money-lenders on down were only too happy to finance ever expanding corporate empire-builders (and their competitors). Though it made for some boom times and generated more income for many people, the long-term result has been too costly in resources, energy, waste, pollution, taxes, health, lives, and quality of life. All that, plus growing populations living those high-maintenance lives and robbing the next generations of their prospects, is what makes it not sustainable. Instead of assisting corporate empire growth, we need government policies reversed to reinforce self-reliance in local ecologically-healthy economies. **This is the third cultural commitment all societies need to make for a healthy, peaceful world.**

The security of owning your home and growing your food or knowing who does enables people to better feel in charge of their lives. Not having to worry about adequate shelter or having enough real food frees people to attain higher purposes that better actualize their mature potential of human functioning. This includes helping younger generations get established.

Keeping investor-owned corporations in secondary roles with a majority of the world's citizens practicing mostly self-reliance in local "green" community economies is the only way to have sustainable health and peace (and only possible if their numbers allow and stay relatively right-sized to each habitat).

In addition to directly providing physical and psychological needs, there are other health reasons for growing our own food and/or buying from local organic growers.

- We have artificial growth hormones in milk from industrial dairies which affect young bodies prematurely. We have steroids and antibiotics in meat from industrial feedlots which result in infections resistant to antibiotics in humans. The residue from herbicides and pesticides on shipped-in food and/or pathogens spread by handlers (who can't afford to stay home if they don't get paid sick leave) can make us ill, terminally ill in the case of cancers from chemicals. This harms tens of thousands of people yearly and costs their families and taxpayers. It also requires taxpayers to pay for costly government inspections or the problems get worse.

- Several research studies have established the presence of some 100 to 200 chemicals in the umbilical cords of newborn babies that are foreign to our evolvement. A similar situation exists with breast milk. It is easy to believe that some of those chemicals are causing impaired brain development, like increasing ADHD and autism, also many childhood and adult cancers.

- Prior to the last 10,000 or so years (when overpopulation of habitats first became the problem), our hunting and gathering ancestors ate a more varied and nutritious diet than we do (including insects). Along with the exercise needed, it made them taller, healthier, and more physically fit. (Today's industrial farming and urbanization has all but killed food diversity and meaningful exercise – our average lifespan is mostly longer because of medical science and largely being compared to people who lived in the last 10,000 years.) In our own gardens and pastures using methods of permaculture (sustainable organic growing), we can get exercise, connection to Nature, and more of the nutritional diversity of diet like our healthier ancestors whose bodies we inherited.

There are also substantial environmental reasons why growing food locally is best.

- Over two thirds (70%) of the world's fresh water use goes for the irrigation of food-growing fields and pastures (the bigger the operation, the more wasteful). Much of this irrigation is from mining underground aquifers beyond their recharging ability. And we have phosphorous from artificial fertilizer runoff creating algae blooms with poisonous toxins making many lakes unusable water sources. This is at a time when we have entered the era of fresh water scarcity in various areas of the planet, including the U.S. Southwest.

- Modern agriculture is getting increasingly expensive (even with government subsidies). We cut down trees and break up sod to make fields for crops. We use large-scale industrial production and harvesting equipment on huge irrigated farms along with artificial fertilizers plus weed and insect poisons. Then we have that produce trucked hundreds of miles to big city supermarkets for purchase and consumption by people driving there. This agricultural system is not only less reliably healthy, hugely inefficient and wasteful, but is also the biggest source of green-house gases (more than all other cars, trucks, boats, and airplanes combined or more than all power plants and factories together).

- We've got methane coming from both ends of every meat animal and from all the rice paddies. We manufacture artificial fertilizer and overuse it (to produce more) which creates nitrous oxide. Both methane and nitrous oxide are many times more potent as greenhouse gases than carbon dioxide.

- Ironically, the greenhouse gases coming mostly from modern agriculture are making the climate more unpredictable for modern agriculture. I say we'd better join those who are going with local, more natural methods of growing food.

Other big considerations for growing your own and/or buying local, organic food (in the U.S.).

- The average age of independent farmers is getting too old to farm and it's too expensive for enough young to take their place. Urban corporate empires are buying up farmlands, then renting them to tenant farmers to work for corporate profits (just like feudal times). We need land trusts and land reform to favor small farms with local ownership.
- Big industrial agricultural producers will only grow what makes them the most profits and sell it where they get the most money. Thus, most of the world depends on just four crops for food, both directly and fed to animals for meat. They are corn, wheat, soybeans, and rice. They can be machine grown, harvested, stored, and shipped most easily on the largest scale (for the most corporate profits). Monocultures like this make many people one extreme-weather event or one plant disease or one insect infestation or one adverse political decision away from serious problems with hunger.
- In any case, with global warming, agronomists also expect the grain harvests to drop 10% for each one degree Celsius rise in average temperature. Growing population, energy costs, climate change, and water shortages say the price of supermarket food can only go up and up.
- Opening up cropland closer to the warming Arctic Circle gets us soils too acidic for grains. Generally speaking, we can't depend on new cropland becoming available to feed our growing population; cultivating what's not already under cultivation makes for too many other too-expensive-to-solve problems.
- Also, surveys show most large cities have only a two or three-day supply of trucked-in food in their stores at any one time. Gangs or terrorists only have to blow up the right highway or bridge or tunnel to create mass chaos and violence among hungry city dwellers dependent on supermarket chains. Today's super-storms can do the same.

Depending on where you live and if you are lucky enough to be employed, you might get a credit union (avoid big banks) to lend you the money with a mortgage to buy land for growing food.

Generally, a mortgage and farming for a living spells trouble. The mortgage holder wants a payment every month – a farm itself will not produce income every month – another source of income is necessary until the mortgage is paid. Before that, you don't actually own the property and interest on the loan adds to the cost. Keep in mind, then, the smaller the mortgage and the sooner you pay it off, the better.

If you don't have much reliable income, remember, it is less expensive to find a small amount of good-enough land and put some shelter on it than to be hunting for a house. Abandoned, non-polluted land or worn-out soil can be built up for growing (keep adding compost) and will be cheaper to acquire. A used travel trailer or mobile home becomes a quicker shelter until you can build yourself a "tiny house," cabin or cottage. Property taxes will be cheaper. (Stupid zoning laws need to be considered.)

One must also be sure that either rainfall or a reliable source of non-polluted water for irrigation is adequate for growing your own food. Water can be stored from rainy seasons, if the best growing temperatures are in dry seasons.

Note that finding good land at cheaper prices will be more possible in areas of declining population. Most young people today are, instead, flocking to artificial, high-maintenance, quick-fix good-feeling habitats (large cities). Considering the future (and gentrification), they would be best off moving into small, dying rural communities which sorely need revitalizing with young energy. Renting or leasing to buy on contract is also more possible there, especially from older citizens ready to share their garden plots with interested and stronger young people.

Beyond acquiring ownership of or rights to food-growing land, some regular income will add to quality living.

Though it can be done, you will have more options for health and development with regular income. Don't be without access to medical care or the Internet. If you can't continue your current employment online or otherwise, create a small business or find local employment. This makes the location of your land important.

Growing extra food to sell at farmers' markets or to grocery stores and restaurants or subscription sales could provide extra income. Learning a necessary skill or craft that no one else is doing in your locality could do it. (Find a need and fill it.) Providing live entertainment for a fee or donations can add to a community's quality of life and your own savings.

Hopefully, there would be no reason to keep expanding your "business" until it runs you. The stress of managing ever-growing, got-to-beat-the-competition businesses would no longer be necessary in stable populations.

Locally owned shops and retail stores in small towns and communities need to be revived. Worker-owned cooperatives could provide better services to local residents, also manufacture equipment and tools that aid garden-farmers. A carbon tax to cut down on fossil fuel use in transportation would slow global warming – and speed up all manner of decentralization of businesses for more local employment.

Remember that there are basically two ways to be comfortable with money – make a lot or not need a lot. To not need a lot and make enough is the most comfortable (and for Mother Earth too).

The exit strategy – a realistic direction for future generations. (Requires persistence, patience, and faith.)

In the past, many cultures had reached high standards of healthful, peaceful, beautiful community living before overpopulation compromised them with ugliness, vulgarity, and violence. I would say the best template for sustainable civilization has societies in which, certainly not all, but the majority of families are living on small organic garden-farms, with separate quarters for grandparents, producing their own food to eat with extra to sell at farmer's markets. These garden-farms would be interspersed with small communities of craft and artisan shops, locally-owned retail stores and cooperatives, local savings and loan banks, worker-owned small factories, small classrooms of health-and-peace-teaching public schools, publically-funded medical/dental clinics, etc. Local solar units would provide most electricity.

Each such "rural" area would surround a modest, totally "green" urban hub, mostly populated with young people and their mentors. These cities would be centers for free higher education, sports, the arts and entertainment, necessary government agencies, and larger, well-regulated benefit corporations manufacturing needed products and appropriate technology.

All organized government would be bottom-up layered (republican) democracies. All net income would be taxed progressively after realistic deductions for essential family expenses of up to two children. With stable populations well educated for health and peace, far, far less tax revenue would be needed for infrastructure and public services. And retired volunteers could maintain and staff much of both.

The rural area around each urban hub would be surrounded and interconnected by wilderness (with wildlife) for climate, environmental, medicinal, genetic, recreational, and spiritual benefits. Most needed wood and metal materials would be "mined" from unneeded and dismantled equipment and buildings.

Continued – moving from unsustainable growth and development to ecologically affordable living.

Young people would be required to put in two years of government service, before or after two or more years of free post-high school artistic, technological, or professional training as socially needed. This would be followed by private or public employment (many instructors and technology tenders required). Many young people could be involved in "safe" sports and in the performing arts for the enjoyment and entertainment of everyone.

When they have paired off and are ready to raise a couple of kids, most young people would move back to a garden-farm (usually one of their parent's), engage themselves in the local economy, volunteer, and be responsible citizens of their community. Someone in each household would still "work" for income, be rewarded with more money for working more and for better ideas and creations. However, expanding production and getting wealthy by today's standards would not make any sense – no extra demand or inflation. People would be into healthy living, relationships, artful expressions of human nature, and Nature's beauty instead of accumulating things.

All communities and their hub city would be connected with small roads suitable for pedestrians, bicycles, and golf-cart size electric cars and trucks. Non-polluting, public-funded mass transit trains (including freight) would also connect more outlying communities with their hub city and with other hubs across continents. Crossing oceans would mostly be by modern dirigibles and sailing ships (no hurry). Jumbo jets, 18-wheelers, monster tankers and container ships as well as skyscrapers, huge malls, and most large buildings would become unaffordable relics from the past, the materials recycled or returned to a natural state.

Local religious organizations would still minister to the community with support groups, volunteer care-givers, and reminders of sustainable, Nature-fitting cultural values. (Nature is the Higher Power – synonymous with God.)

I don't know that it's going to happen; I do believe it needs to happen before the end of this century.

We know from past history and present science that the above model can work indefinitely if coupled with human populations reduced and then stabilized to carrying capacities of natural habitats. We also know that low-stress living, simple pleasures, and expectations that match reality result in the most happiness, health, and peace. There can be many variations (sub-cultures) within this model, of course, that would still provide the physical and psychological benefits of mostly self-reliant lifestyles in local economies.

I repeat – there are five areas of knowledge (that first root of civilization) required for universal, sustainable health and peace as determined by science. (1) How to take care of oneself physically and psychologically. (2) How to do that AND get along with other people. (3) How to do those two AND conduct oneself in bottom-up democracy. (4) How to do those three AND live ecologically on planet Earth. (5) How to do all of the above AND be an effective parent, mentor, and good example to the next generations. (These five areas should have a higher priority than STEM courses per se.)

Note that the world-wide teaching of self-reliant knowledge gets more possible when there are less people to teach. Note that less people make more suitable land, fresh water, other resources, and more local (decentralized) business opportunities available. Note that less people erase the incentives to build empires to get between people and their needs, thus destroying self-reliance. And there would be no reason to resent paying taxes on surplus income (the incentives would be to share and donate).

With a mostly self-reliant lifestyle in a bottom-up democratic, right-sized community of other self-reliant practitioners, you are free to be yourself. You can live according to values scientifically known to be conducive to health and peace. You don't have to prostitute yourself, that is, do things with your body that you wouldn't do if money (or survival) were not involved.

Connecting the Dots – The Failed System

Human sexuality without complete (sex) education
> Leads to

Overpopulation of natural human habitats
> Leads to

Competition for resources and learning opportunities
> Leads to

Political-corporate-religious empire-building to out-compete
> Leads to

Power-addicted, autocratic leaders and dependent followers
> Leads to

Class, ethnic, racial, economic, and military warfare
> Leads to

A world of unsustainable, unstable, ugly, destructive environments, poverty, violence, and terrorism, ever increasing fear, hate, suffering, and premature dying.

(Note that, once the system is established, going up is also true.)

Connecting the Dots – The Successful System

Human sexuality with complete (sex) education
    Leads to
Right-sized populations of natural human habitats
    Leads to
Cooperation with resources and learning opportunities
    Leads to
Social conditions maintained by bottom-up democracies
    Leads to
Freely self-actualizing, self-reliant, diverse and mature people
    Leads to
Collaborative, values-united communities and nations
    Leads to
A sustainably healthy and beautiful, just and peaceful world.

(Note that, once the system is established, going up is also true.)

(Also note – this system is up and running in more and more areas of the world. The big challenges are expanding awareness and choices to all the world's people and overcoming the "pushback" by empire-aligned corporate, religious, and political conservatives financially and psychologically profiting from the status quo.)

Summary of recommendations for young people. The future is in your hands.

- Keep a life-long learning habit pursuing truth and reality, including what in this book might be inaccurate. I am sincere, but also human. Be open to changing your mind when data and evidence indicate otherwise.
- Support and promote everywhere the necessity of public schools with qualified teachers in small-enough classrooms of students to be learning the ways of health and peace.
- Take stock of, build up, and maintain your support system, that is, your learned habits and routines, your physical health, and your relationships so as to have more psychological energy (will-power) to contribute to a healthier more peaceful society. You also need this psychological strength for faith, hope, and optimism.
- Follow *The Legacy Rule.* *"To best love your children, create no more or no more than one or two."* Spread and promote it everywhere, repeatedly.
- Advocate and support access to contraception and family planning at every opportunity. (A good family planning motto = *"One is good, two is enough, if outnumbered then stop."*
- Get as close to living an ecologically-defensible life as you can in health and peace, especially with waste-stream pollution, your consumption of resources, and emissions of greenhouse gases. Support organizations promoting this.
- Get more free of reliance on any empire-building organizations by getting as self-reliant as you can with water, food, shelter, health, clothes, energy, transportation, and access to education and information.

Continued recommendations for young people.

- In this overpopulated (and nuclear) age, we cannot afford opposing narratives (stories) about who is entitled to what parts of planet Earth. Support and promote the only story big enough (and important enough) to include everyone – the necessity of us all living in science-backed harmony with Nature, thus restoring and protecting Mother Earth.

- Keep informed about politics, legislation proposed, and threats to democracy by empire-builders. Demand transparency in public institutions and quality news reporting. Your best bet for real ongoing information is public news services and a free, not privatized, non-commercially controlled Internet.

- Vote and volunteer, support candidates for public office that you think are worthy. Give your government officials and legislatures feedback, especially when you agree with them – most people only do so when they disagree. (This happens while lobbyists are giving them lots of positive attention.)

- Regularly thank public, corporate, and religious officials who "get it." Persistently seek to enlighten, petition, and demonstrate against those who don't – always respectfully and peacefully.

- Support with your presence, votes, labor, and money those organizations that are rightly engaged in furthering health and peace, locally and throughout the world.

- Nowadays, living so many years can mean an elderly person is more out of touch, at least, with technology and the competition. Don't write off old people. Before overpopulation set in, they were largely revered for the wisdom that comes with living so many years. Most still have some.

- Elderly people can become social burdens at a time when there are too many social burdens. (Be gentle with us – the precedents you set may follow you as your years go by.)

Some lessons required for sustainable health and peace.

1. That the Earth is not flat; it is a self-regulating biosphere maintaining finite requirements for life.
2. That the sun does not revolve around the Earth; the Earth revolves around the sun, like a spaceship carrying its own life-supports.
3. That all the Earth's species, including human beings, were created through evolutionary processes over millions of years involving natural selection of the most adaptable individuals and cooperative groups.
4. That neither might makes right nor repetition makes truth.
5. That being wrong is not failure when it elevates us to a new level of understanding. (Competition devalues this with "losers.")
6. That traditions should never trump evidence and logic. Knowledge needs to trump traditions, also change lifestyles.
7. That the pursuit of truth and knowledge of reality should be a higher value than winning power and control. Knowledge should determine authority, not vice versa.
8. That the Earth does not belong to us; we belong to the Earth. It is not ours to greedily plunder, but to respectfully enjoy its blessings (and act like trustees of our descendants' future).
9. That neither vows of chastity, nor "bad" reputations, nor threats of being stoned to death or going to eternal hell-fire do a very good job of preventing people from being sexual.
10. That for humans to go forth and multiply is now an obsolete and dangerous dictum; there are no more habitats to which Earthlings can go forth and, where they have already gone, ever decreasing resources for them to divide.

11. That when people get their sexual needs met, starting with complete sex education, they do best at practicing safe and responsible sex compared to those who are kept sexually ignorant and/or deprived.

12. That a complete sex education will include the evils of overpopulation and the current need to reduce human populations to scientifically determined, sustainable carrying capacities of natural human habitats.

13. That the first three to five years of a child's life are when 90% of the brain is organized (mapped or hardwired) with the pathways that set the stage and make the emotional connections for life's future learning – some future lessons will be easier, some future lessons more difficult. (Mostly shame and fear connections can make a different future than mostly love and trust, for example.)

14. That two parents with an only child mean much more parental nurturing and teaching time plus four grandparents to help socialize, care for, and educate him or her. And good friends in similar situations can be "recruited" for the benefits of extended families and playmates (like uncles, aunts, and cousins).

15. That while humans have always altered their environment for convenience, safety, and stimulation, the real issue is how many humans can do so in a given habitat without making it unhealthy and ecologically dysfunctional.

16. That overpopulation is not so much about everybody having enough space. Overpopulation is more about how their numbers with their collective activities can change the climate, decrease other life supports, cause need-less suffering, even end human life on Earth.

17. That in addition to running out of fresh water, we may reach a shortage of phosphorous for the amount of artificial fertilizer we use to grow the food we need.

18. That to truly, sustainably maximize universal health and peace, we each need to use the Earth's resources in ways that allow all others (including future others) to do likewise if they wish – only possible with sufficient knowledge and right-sized populations.
19. That to have sustainability, we have to have continuity between generations and not have big empire-building corporations creating separate cultures of values between them (like in entertainment, fashions, technology) to sell more "product" and make more profits.
20. That there is no such thing as waste in Nature's cycles. Nothing can ever really be thrown away – everything has to go somewhere in a form, amount, and at a rate that Nature can use if we are to have sustainability. Too many people make this impossible.
21. That two of the most cherished beliefs in U.S. culture – unlimited population growth and forever economic development – are not grounded in scientific evidence. They are not even logical.
22. That our spiritual practice is what we each do every day (rituals and routines) to center ourselves, connect with the wholeness of life, and feel okay in the world around us. This is best done with natural surroundings. (Our early hunting and gathering ancestors had no word for nature separate from their word for humans.) Our spiritual practice should leave us in "good spirits" – a mindful, peaceful state at one with Nature (God).
23. That many people today are so trained by big business that their spiritual practice is to awaken with alarm, rush or skip breakfast, fight traffic to beat it to work, and use a drug (caffeine) to get through it all, then alcohol or marijuana to relax afterward. On weekends they catch up on home life with the same urgency, but may attend religious services for some spiritual help, then go back to business as usual during the week.

24. That religion, by definition, is based on constructs and concepts that cannot be tested with scientific methods. As such, religious constructs and concepts can never be universally embraced like knowledge and should never be frozen into laws. That's a set-up for conflict with those who think or feel differently.

25. That words do not have fixed meanings – not in sacred books, not in translations, not in wise constitutions. The meanings of words may be what speakers or writers intend them to be at the time, but "times" change. As insights and wisdoms change through generations the meanings of relevant words can change too. Conservative minds feel best with some important matters fixed for all time. However, evolving knowledge can call for changes and new adaptations to those same matters.

26. That faith is what we believe and knowledge is what we know and it is best to be open to change what we believe when new knowledge reveals otherwise.

27. That knowledge is fact-based and that faith-based knowledge is an oxymoron. Faith is important for what we don't know and for hope, given what we do know.

28. That for sustainable civilization, we need individuals socialized and educated to be responsible for themselves to the extent that they are able. We also need individuals and collective society helping those who are not able, and everybody (even CEOs of private corporations) taking responsibility for maintaining the social and environmental conditions that sustainably allow for both functions to be done.

29. That individualism is a problem if individuals believe that "what I do will not make a difference given what everyone else is doing." A sense of personal morality (it's the right thing to do) is necessary to counteract this. Otherwise, if enough people believe that what they do as individuals will not matter much (like peeing in the ocean of humanity), we develop collective problems.

30. That, generally speaking, people pull together to solve problems when they see it is in their own interest. In the case of overpopulation and greenhouse gases, it can be too late by the time they realize it. This argues for the right education and ongoing information up front to maintain moral consciousness about the environment.

31. That our early social and physical environments make our habits and our habits make our future social and physical environments and this relationship determines whether or not we live a life of mostly health and peace (and pass the same off to our descendants). Profits cannot determine this.

32. That there is a difference between education focused on making money and education focused on the healthiest, most peaceful ways to live sustainably.

33. That most U.S. voters are fugitives from reality – seduced or driven away by corporate, political, and religious empires who own or buy time on commercial broadcasting and communications systems.

34. That we need all people to value logic and a sense of reality and be able to better tell the difference between what's factual and what's myth, propaganda, fantasy, and illusion.

35. That people are continuously making decisions in response to social problems. The issue is whether escaping reality, distractions by shopping/buying, taking pills, drinking, doing drugs, etc. are better than attacking with knowledge, ability, and will power. The former adds a lot more to the economy, but . . .

36. That one of the biggest benefits of more education is increased ability to distinguish, or differentiate, or discriminate between variables in causes and consequences so as to make better decisions in matters of personal and collective health and peace. Most genuine reality will be found in between supposedly obvious black or white, good or bad, right or wrong – except when it's not – and it can change.

37. That among the main points of a good education are experiencing the joy of discovery, the excitement of new insight, the pleasure in creative work, the value of greater discernment, the boundaries for living in maximum health and peace, and how to psychologically mature and grow in self-reliance.

38. That anytime we allow our public education and information systems to deteriorate to save taxes, we simply multiply the amount of tax money needed for legislation and welfare, also law enforcement, courts, prisons, military preparedness, and meeting a host of other problems later, even to next generations.

39. That the smartest human being in any specialty is too ignorant if that's all he or she knows. We live in a system of interdependent relationships which calls for a liberal education before specializing.

40. That taxpayers providing a free education to each person, including two years of community college, and especially focused on knowledge for living in sustainable health and peace (with complete sex education), is far cheaper than supporting a lifetime of welfare or crime or prison with offspring most likely on the same path.

41. That democracy is only as effective as the education and information level of its voters (the big problem in newly emerging democracies). Support free public education, free public information broadcasting, and free Internet around the globe.

42. That world-wide relevant, secular education and information to young people (independent of any religious, corporate, or political ideology) has the best chance of changing political, religious, cultural, and economic traditions incompatible with health and peace.

43. That the slogan, Freedom is not free – support our troops," is not as important as, "Freedom is not free – support universal education and ongoing information." This is so people do not need to spend much tax-money on troops and troops do not have to put their lives on the line.

44. That every fact, statement, and event can be interpreted positively or negatively depending on one's biases or an organization's publicity (public manipulation) goals.

45. That the Fairness Doctrine (all credible sides of issues have to be presented) should be returned (Reagan banned it as part of deregulation). This best governs all private broadcasters of political and governmental news to control for their inherent commercial conflicts of interest. Since then certain cable TV "news" channels and radio talk shows have been creating their own market following by using news selection, spin, and innuendo to confirm the biases of "low information" voters. They now have the U.S. Congress (and the entire country) so polarized that nothing gets done to rein in big corporations and solve problems.

46. That as long as corporate empire-builders are in control of your news media, they will be trying to give you the news that makes you want to read, watch, and listen by appealing to your biases and using cheap sensationalism to arouse your curiosity. They will be conveying importance to outrageous politicians. They will be creating controversy when none exists. (It's about being able to sell advertising.)

47. That even in politics, if the wealthy elite control communications and information, they can create doubt, fear, and anger to get the uninformed and misinformed helping to make them better off by voting for the wrong persons and against their own interests.

48. That if they are set up independent of political leadership, public-funded reporting of news will likely be the most free of political bias, religious ideology, or corporate propaganda.

49. That the biggest problem with living in a big city may be the lack of reality checks with Nature and where real food comes from and how it can be sustainably produced to maximize health of body and soil.

50. That there will be differences in values learned when growing up in competitive and over-crowded cities amid concrete from the ground up and mostly occupying one's self with artificial stimulation, compared to growing up with free-range exploration in small cohesive and cooperative communities with local economies amid natural settings. Some of these values are more conducive to sustainability than others.

51. That the bigger the city, the more ecologically costly its maintenance and thus the more challenging its sustainability. The larger a city gets, the more grossly inefficient it will be for keeping sufficient food going in, waste coming out, and contagious diseases from spreading. (Even my favorite city, Paris, is heavily subsidized by the rest of the French – thank you, by the way.)

52. That abundant wilderness areas (as in undeveloped) are necessary to civilization because they moderate climate, stimulate rainfall, function as carbon sinks, build up soil, hold moisture, control run-off and stop erosion, provide habitat for wildlife and genetic material for medicines, also function as Earthly reality checks, places for recreation and spiritual rejuvenation.

53. That liberals have the largest comfort zone and conservatives the narrowest and neither is always good or always bad. (It depends on the issue and the times.)

54. That liberals need to keep aware of individual responsibilities for self-determination and conservatives need to keep aware that social opportunities are necessary for individuals to learn those responsibilities.

55. That liberals are best at recognizing the need for change and handling diversity while conservatives are best at recognizing uniting values and keeping them viable. We need both perspectives in a democratic-republic. However, to stay great, a great country has to make changes as conditions change.

56. That it is not very wise of citizens to expect solutions to the nation's and world's problems from people who benefit most from the status quo. (The rich should never be allowed more power over policy than the non-rich.)
57. That the U.S. really has two separate economies – the top 20% who have made nearly all the gains since 1980 (with conservatives, to date, in control of the Presidency and/or Congress three-fourths of the time) and the 80% whose incomes have been stagnant or falling in purchasing power since then.
58. That Nature and human nature thrive on diversity. In Nature, diversity guarantees life sustainability somewhere. Diversity in human nature guarantees the best ideas somewhere to rise to the top (and be improved along the way). Bottom-up democracy handles diversity. Top-down rulers kill diversity by homogenizing a culture so its people are easier to control. (Passing standardized tests to get somewhere in the corporate world does it. A state religion really does it – it's backed by God.)
59. That the development of most technology is prompted by trying to live with too many people and that quality of life is less about technology and more about what makes for sustainable health, peace, liberty, justice, and love in our relationships.
60. That, as far as their natural evolvement is concerned, humans are basically the same now as they were 10,000 years ago. There is only so much technology and products people can use for comfort, convenience, and stimulation without it becoming too foreign and detrimental to their physical and psychological well-being.
61. That the parents are primarily responsible for raising a child, but it is not realistic to hold them solely responsible. It does take a village (society) to raise children and corporations have to be made legally part of that contract.

62. That sugar in all its forms is the real "gateway" drug. Unlike complex carbohydrates, its effect on the brain's reward system is similar, just far more subtle than hard drugs or even marijuana. With simple carbs, we crave more. We eat more. Corporate empires in the food industry like this. They've added sugar to 80% of (U.S.) supermarket foods in spite of obesity, diabetes, and heart disease rates (and they once fought the labeling of ingredients). The amorality of big corporations leads to big government.

63. That the more competition for resources and opportunities because of overpopulation, the more institutional government is needed. The more cooperation between people because of right-sized population the less institutional government is needed.

64. That power-mongers and their empires are like leaches or predators on the people. In a secular democracy, you can vote them out of government and vote in alternatives. On the other hand, private corporate empires, intent on making ever more money any way possible, cannot exactly be voted out of business. It's wise to make sure you don't need them to live, also to pressure government officials to adequately regulate them.

65. That we are entering an age when most every piece of technology we use can be secretly sending data about who we are and what we do back to the big private, for-profit corporations who made it. That they might use it to tempt and manipulate and control us with more technology or sell the information to others for the same reasons is a good bet (or to employers). Technology is supposed to make our lives easier and more relaxing. Rather, it's making us more available to advertising and salespersons, also bosses. (And they're trying to teach us to just be afraid of big government.)

66. That the mother of all slippery slopes is competition between people for livelihood, especially competition between corporate empires with absentee owners (stockholders). All such competition needs rules and referees and that means government.

67. That more "free-market" capitalism is recommended (and only works) in local economies in which business owners live where they do business. They will have consciences and care about their personal reputations, their neighbors, and their community (and sustainability).

68. That so-called free-market capitalism (by their rules) is not recommended (and does not work) for huge private corporate empires in state and national and global economies. Leaders and the many scattered investor-owners have no personal connection or stake in the relationships and the communities impacted by their decisions.

69. That, when it involves huge corporate conglomerates, free markets may regulate selling prices, but will not regulate costs of production. Competitors, to stay competitive, will end up operating at the bottom of any ethical scale they can to increase profits. It becomes law-of-the-jungle capitalism. The weak and the young (start-ups) get eaten, workers and consumers get exploited, and waste is dropped in powerless people's back yards (or streams or air-sheds). We also have corporations with anonymous front and shell companies making secret deals with corrupt government officials, hiding assets and income, stealing resources from the citizens of poor countries, etc. (Check out "Global Witness.")

70. That charging interest on debt was once considered a sin (still is in Islam?) and now U.S. federal monetary policy is corporate-designed to discourage savings and encourage debt among citizens for that purpose. Debt and interest on debt are used to pull income away from the many laboring people (working and middle classes) into the hands of the relatively few already wealthy. The same is true with U.S. lending to developing nations. (At this writing, the policy is "working well.")

71. That the bigger and stronger corporate empires get, with their attorneys and CPAs and lobbyists always finding ways to increase profits, the bigger and stronger government has to get with attorneys and accountants and enforcers to regulate them. Sooner or later, one way or another, the people (taxpayers) can't afford them. (Then corporations use their power to help elect candidates running on the "cut taxes" sentiment to escape regulation.)

72. That "people would be lazy and good-for-nothing if they didn't have to work to live" is a myth believed and perpetuated by competitive mentalities who need people working for them. People who don't have to concern themselves with lower-order needs (water, food, shelter, safety) will have natural curiosity and incentives for higher-order behaviors like pursuing knowledge, creating art, and contributing to society. Look at all the currently "retired" people who do it.

73. That abundance, efficiency, safety, health, security, democracy, education, liberty, happiness, justice, peace, and sustainability would all be increased by reducing the world's human population. The profits of big corporate-empires would decrease accordingly. What a sacrifice we make for their existence.

74. That for economies to continue indefinitely, the Earth's environment and ecology and social-psychological goals of wellness and peace between individuals, communities, and nations, have to take higher priority than profits.

75. That any modern overpopulated society can be understood on a continuum of people with the largest comfort zones on one end and those with the narrowest on the other. The most educated and liberal will be at the most secure end and the lesser or narrowest educated will be at the least secure end. They are most likely to be manipulated by empire-builders using fear and anger (and will own the most guns).

76. That when most citizens fall in the middle of such a security continuum (as in middle class), it will best hold society together. If economic policies (think Reaganomics) shrink the middle class, then more and more people will fall to the insecure end leaving fewer and fewer people feeling secure. (And the NRA becomes the fourth branch of government.)

77. That in the U.S., the issue is not whether individuals have a right to defend themselves against bad guys. Of course, they do. The issue is what weapons will the bad guys have? Any weapon we allow to be developed and sold in the public marketplace will inevitably fall into their hands. Where do we draw the line? So far, we have gone from single-shot muskets and pistols to AK 47s. Next?

78. That gun-manufacturing corporations will contribute to anti-tax politicians, in part, so that public law enforcement agencies have limited budgets and can only offer so much public protection.

79. That 98% of all gun deaths in the U.S. are suicides, homicides, or accidents, plus 1% unknown. That's a lot of "collateral damage" for the convenience of gun control laws with loop holes. Support gun-owner background checks, licenses, and bullet tracing registration. That's not the same as banning guns and will save a lot of lives, grief, and taxpayer money (easier law enforcement).

80. That the U.S. gun-manufacturing corporations, with their NRA scare tactics, have a sure-fire business model when it comes to self-defense. They sell guns to insecure people to protect themselves, but make sure there are loopholes in any gun-laws so that criminals and crazies can still easily get them. So there are mass shootings every month, the news media does their part, more people get insecure, and the market for self-defense just keeps growing. This business model is also used by corporate empires making weapons of war to sell to nations and their enemies. (And the United States' weapons industry leads the world by far in this trafficking.)

81. That there is a difference between government and administration of government. Administering government can be inefficient for many reasons. One is if it is bloated with more revenue and more personnel than is needed (think Pentagon or Department of Agriculture). Another is not enough budget revenue to hire enough personnel for the amount of work to do (think EPA or IRS). Still another is when the salaries of administrators are too low to attract very capable administrators from the pool.

82. That the range of income tax rates in the U.S. once ranged from 0 to 91% and that's when the rising economic tide lifted all boats. Along with a healthy estate tax, there was no growing gap between the 20% wealthiest and the 80% everybody else. (We elected more liberal politicians in both parties then.)

83. That in general, the countries with the least happy and healthy people and the most dysfunctional governments also have the lowest taxes in the world and the countries with the happiest, healthiest people and best functioning governments have the highest (also fewer billionaires).

84. That instead of putting ever more taxpayer's money into defense contracts with corporate empire-builders, we should be providing free higher education, building mass transit and renewable energy systems, and rebuilding our nations' electrical grids, water systems, and sanitation systems.

85. That the United States, for all its good-hearted people, its past progressive ideas, its brilliant engineering feats, and its humanitarian contributions to the world, is now a backward nation in many respects, thanks to 30 years of ascending far right political resistance to progressive taxes and change. It's shocking college tuition system, its incomprehensible population policy, its obscene financial inequality, its inhumane medical care system (controlled by for-profit corporations), its embarrassing mass transit system, its crumbling infrastructure, its fixation on guns and violence: all have made us the wonder of the world (not in a good way).

86. That wars are not ended by possessing more ships and planes or bigger guns and bombs. Because war creates more rigid hard-liners, vengeful radicals, and greedy profiteers, truly ending a war can take decades, even centuries. Wars are ended by winning hearts and minds to policies that promote health and peace; more importantly, they are prevented the same way.

87. That organizations like Earth Policy Institute have the numbers that show we could move the world economy off the path of decline and collapse and onto sustainability for less than 1/3 of the U. S. Pentagon's annual budget – if we had the political will (or more informed voters writing or riding our politicians).

88. That the best health insurance is an individual's knowledge and habits (and opportunities) for taking care of him or her self and beyond that we should have universal, single-payer government medical insurance, also local public medical corps to hold down total costs.

89. That medical care should be seen as a right for all citizens, not just those with enough money to pay for medical insurance and that it should include coverage for contraception and morning-after pills.

90. That for the Social Security program to be sustainable in the U.S., the income level cap on paying into the fund needs to be removed and the income level on who receives payments needs to be capped (the opposite of now). It should be managed like insurance, a pay-it-forward risk pool by which younger working generations subsidize only older retired generations who need it with the younger knowing they will have the same safety net if needed when they are old. Not making these changes is another way politicians are harming the health and peace of the next generations.

91. That Gross Domestic Product (GDP) is a grossly misleading indicator of economic health. It was conceived under the myth of perpetual abundance. It ignores social capital, resource depletion, and environmental damage. It also leaves out the "work" that Nature does for us, like climate moderation, flood control, pest control, water purification, insect pollination, carbon sequestering, soil conservation, nutrient cycling, and seed dispersal.

92. That GDP does not apply in a shrinking population economy where prosperity means more quality of living, not quantity of stuff. Growth will be in scientific knowledge, humanities education, functional intelligence, physical and psychological health, supportive relationships, morality, justice, liberty, and the arts. Something like a Sustainable Well-Being Index is needed. (Study the nation of Bhutan.)

93. That the most deserving heroes to the next generations will be leaders who were active in making right-sized population and environmental progress. So far, the most environmentally progressive presidents in the U.S. have been Republicans Theodore Roosevelt and Richard Nixon (not exactly a hero otherwise) and Democrats Jimmy Carter and Barack Obama (though most of his efforts were blocked by Far Right Republicans). FDR and LBJ were also good for the environment.

94. U.S. presidents with the worst environmental records (and otherwise) are Republicans Ronald Reagan and George W. Bush (with the help of extremist VP, Dick Cheney). They also cost future taxpayers by cutting taxes while increasing military spending – the latter with two long, useless wars when he should have simply joined NATO intelligence resources to get Osama bin Laden. The bottom-line cause of the 9/11 horror was too many people per habitat carrying capacities in the Middle East. (1918 and 1953 empire-building by Britain and the U.S. didn't help.) What if just a tenth of those 3 trillion dollars (and counting) had gone to spreading science-based health and peace education, building infrastructure, and providing contraception instead?

95. That as the upheaval and confusion of world population reduction escalates one way or another, the people best off will be self-reliant in local economies.

96. That when all people can grow up with basic needs met (water, food, shelter, security, acceptance, love, sex, natural space, and the relevant knowledge that makes it all sustainable), we can put our faith and trust in we, the people, to want to and be able to live together in health and peace.

97. That with modern smart phones, everybody can be a journalist and a pundit recording and/or commenting on events as they happen and instantly sending both around the world on Internet social media. That, plus instant access to all the storage of such from others as well as all the past information (and misinformation) stored, can rightly leave us overwhelmed and confused or downright lost as to matters of living well. It is hoped that this book has covered the framework or models that best lend themselves to organizing all this raw material into the most meaningful, purposeful, and satisfying lives.

98. That each of us, without waiting to be led, can join the millions of people at the "grass-roots" level who are already open to learning and working toward a reality-based healthy and peaceful civilization. It is now the largest progressive movement the world has ever known. It requires changing the prevailing economic direction that ever bigger and faster and more things and services with ever more people to buy them is the way to go. That system can probably only be changed by most of us at the bottom doing the changing.

99. And let us believe; let us have faith that there is still time.

Homework Assignment

Go online to either dreamstime.com or bigstockphoto.com and find their photo collections.

Type in the following search words one at a time in the search bars and look at the pictures that come up.

1. overpopulation
2. street crowds or street congestion
3. beach crowds or crowded beaches
4. traffic jams
5. landfills or garbage dumps
6. polluted air
7. polluted water, polluted beaches, or ocean pollution
8. slums or congested housing
9. homelessness
10. hunger or starvation

Then ask yourself the following questions:

"Can we really continue to expand our impact on our planet?"

"What will or how will we stop this ongoing perversion of the gift of life?"

"The trouble with the public is that there is too much of it," said Don Marquis (and he lived from 1878-1937). More people have been born on planet Earth since his death than all of human history before that.

I repeat!

Unsustainable practices lead to evil and collapse. Genetically, that is not who we are and we have had people fighting evil, sometimes more, sometimes less, for the last 10,000 or more years. While goodness has often triumphed, not enough people understand how evil generates to keep it from recycling. The bottom-line answer to every social problem is not more guns or readiness for war. It is not more religious fervor. It is not more prisons, longer sentences, or more executions. It is not more medication. It is not more technology. The bottom-line answer to every social problem is our ability to scientifically investigate, learn, correct obsolete beliefs, change dysfunctional social and ecological habits, and teach evolving knowledge from generation to generation. And we must monitor the consequences of both our traditions and our progressions.

In order for the human species to survive beyond this century, the world-wide implementation of any and all antidotes to all human-caused evils is imperative. But the highest priority goals every community, state, and nation needs to be working on are:

1. Getting science-based reality education and continuous information relevant to health and peace reaching all citizens of the planet, especially young people,
2. Bringing human populations back in balance with the scientifically-determined indefinite carrying capacities of natural human habitats as per *The Legacy Rule*, and
3. Furthering the practice of sustainable self-reliance, including mostly local permaculture (organic) food and (non-polluting) energy production in community economies governed by bottom-up democracy, geared to quality of life with well-regulated, investor and worker-owned benefit corporations public-charter guided to serve the common good first and foremost.

FINAL EXAM

Which society is truly sustainable in health and peace?

1. Its people work for a top-down centralized governing body and are "taken care of" (like children) by that (parental or "nanny") central authority.

2. Its people are slaves to a fear-enforced theocracy or autocracy with limited freedom of inquiry or expression while being continuously indoctrinated on what to think and do.

3. Its behind-the-scenes leaders and profit-minded investors keep more than enough working-age people competing for corporate jobs with just enough pay (fighting inflation) to maintain consumer-spending economies. This is done while they maintain strong militaries to fight over, intimidate, and exploit territory for resources to keep that economy going. Its left-out young people make do with religion, drugs, and welfare or join gangs to fight over, intimidate, and exploit territory for drug, sex-trafficking, kidnapping, or extortion-based economies. And its habitats grow more unnatural, ugly, unhealthy, and dangerous.

4. Its people are working mostly in local "green" economies, valuing science (especially social science), providing health and peace education for all, keeping each other politically informed with civil dialogue, participating in democratic-republican government, living modestly in self-reliance, organically growing most of their own food, cleanly producing their own energy, sharing their blessings, enjoying close relationships and Nature, delighting in the arts and humanities, safely taking pleasure in their sexuality, and following *The Legacy Rule*.

**If we believe it is too idealistic or too late,
it will be too idealistic and too late.**

Earth Citizenship

More people breeding,
　　More competition making,
　　More resources extracting,
　　More waste spewing,
More hell generating.

Family planning,
　　Cooperative thinking,
　　Modest living,
　　Waste-stream recycling,
Heavenly Earth shaping.

The difference is knowing,

On which you are working.

J. Nathan

"Anyone who has ever struggled with poverty knows how extremely expensive it is to be poor."
James Baldwin

"Poverty . . . Not until I knew for certain where my next meal would come from could I give myself up to ignoring that next meal; I could think of other things."
Helen Westley

"Everybody is entitled to their own opinions, but not their own facts."

Daniel Patrick Moynihan

"If something cannot go on forever, it will stop."

Herbert Stein

Good relations, time, and health
Constitute the greatest wealth.

J. Nathan

"A society grows great when old men plant trees whose shade they know they will never sit in."

Greek Proverb

"Our greatest responsibility is to be good ancestors."

Jonas Salk

Environmentalists make the best ancestors.
Family-planning parents make the best ancestors.
The Legacy Rule makes the best ancestors.

"One of the greatest dignities of humankind
is that each successive generation is invested
in the welfare of each new generation."
Fred (Mr.) Rogers

"We have the duty to hope"
Barbara Ward
Eden Project

"That it only comes but once,
Is what makes life so sweet."
Emily Dickenson

The final ending?

Send feedback to thelegacyrule@gmail.com
Follow me on facebook.com/jerry.nathan.988
Or Twitter – Jerry Nathan @TheLegacyRule

CPSIA information can be obtained
at www.ICGtesting.com
Printed in the USA
FFOW03n1854041216
29890FF